"There's an old saying

knocked down in life,
back up'. *What You*
teaches us to reach
through some tough times and encourages us to get back up and start over again, with an unstoppable spirit that refuses to be denied.

"Debra Jones, using her own life experiences, gives us an inside look at the character and courage that one must have in order to face the challenges of life—to reap the tremendous abundance that we all rightly deserve."

Les Brown
nationally acclaimed speaker, TV personality
and author of *Live Your Dreams*

"No matter which road you've walked on during your own special life journey, chances are Debra Jones was right behind you. Sometimes she was jogging . . . and sometimes "limping" just like most of us do. Through her honesty and razor-sharp wit and wisdom you'll not only get to know this remarkable woman, you will recognize yourself. Take a good long look. I know you will like what you see!"

Suzie Humphreys
popular motivational speaker and Dallas, Texas
radio personality

WHAT YOU WANT, WANTS YOU

How to Get Out of Your Rut

Debra Jones

What You Want, Wants You

Second Printing
Published by:
Hark & Associates
225 S. Brady
Claremore, OK 74017

www.DebraJonesOnline.com

Printed in the United States of America.

ISBN 0-9717753-1-1

First Printing by Health Communications, Inc., 1995
Second Printing by Hark & Associates, 2002

Also by Debra Jones
Published by Hark & Associates:

FROM THIN AIR TO MILLIONAIRE

Dedication

This book is dedicated to my family. First to Doug, my wonderful husband and soulmate, with whom I blissfully share this life, thank you for all your support and encouragement. Thank you for allowing me to be me, separate from you. Most of all, thank you for sharing your specialness with me. You are a rare man and I cherish having you in my life.

Secondly, to my children, Joy and Andrew. The two of you are so precious to me. You remind me every day what's truly important about life. I am blessed to have you as my children.

How will you feel when life's run out
About all the things you just thought about?
And when your life's completely through,
What would you want them to say about you?
To ponder, to question, to wonder why . . .
Don't wait to live until it's time to die!

Debra Jones

Contents

Foreword

Debra Jones is a radiant beam of love, wisdom and illumination. She eradicates darkness with the light of her words, deeds and actions. If the candle called your life has been blown out, flamed out or burned out for any reason whatsoever, Debra's words will reignite your candle and encourage you to light the candles of others.

Debra is unique and beautiful inside and out. She has discovered her personal magnificence and awakens you totally to your own. She is fully alive spiritually, mentally and physically, and teaches by example what is possible if you're fully tuned in and turned on.

Debra and I have been friends for years. I've seen her work professionally and she leads with vision, skill, charisma, charm and absolute dedication. As a mother and a wife she is extraordinary. She loves her husband and her two children unconditionally. Our children play together at conferences and conventions around the world, and that has given us time together to walk, talk, think and metaphorically let our hair down. She's authentic and an on-purpose parent.

What I appreciate about her most is that she works full time on developing herself. She constantly increases her self-worth and thereby her net worth. Her personal value is improving at a quantum rate. I watch her work from the platform every couple of years and marvel at the vast improvement in her ability to communicate with the audience. She is increasingly articulate, persuasive and compelling. What she says makes sense, and she paints pictures with words that invite you to expand and improve personally and professionally while challenging you to raise your own standards.

When Debra learns something, she personally bests it! That which works, she shares, making everyone better off and no one worse off. Ancient wisdom teaches us to listen to people who demonstrate what they teach by looking at their results. Debra's results speak for themselves. She's deeply spiritual, happily married and her business enterprises are thriving. Not one to rest on her laurels, her plans for the future are exciting and inviting.

I love everything about this book: the writing, the structure, the philosophy. I can hear Debra's dynamic voice loud and clear in every sentence. I love all the great messages of hope, empowerment and encouragement, and the promises for ever-brighter tomorrows. Mostly, I am ecstatic about the new results you, the reader, will achieve as you apply the insights.

While vacationing in Kona, Hawaii, with my family and neighbor friends, I took this wonderful book and read it at the beach. Our neighbor commented that she didn't know what she wanted. I said, "Have I got the book for you; it's called *What You Want, Wants You*. I loaned her this book and she achieved immediate life-transforming results.

I share this story with you because that's the magic that happened with our books in the *Chicken Soup for the Soul* series, now #1 and #2 on *The New York Times* bestseller list: one person saying to another, "You've got to read this book." I believe the book you're holding will experience the same wonderful fate—word of mouth to best seller.

Walt Disney said, "For a product to succeed big, it has to do three things: be unique, have great word of mouth and have flair. *What You Want, Wants You* meets all three criteria. It's like a potato chip—once you start you can't stop (reading it)! The ideas are memorable, easily transferable and immediately applicable. You'll have a whole new outlook on life after reading this marvelous book.

Mark Victor Hansen
Coauthor of The *New York Times* bestselling series
Chicken Soup for the Soul

Acknowledgments

Life is full and wonderful when we have numerous teachers along the way who are willing to share themselves, their talents and their experiences with us. I am very fortunate to have had a number of such people in my life.

Many people have shaped and influenced me and it is time to recognize them now. My mother, Betty, a strong, loving woman who taught me the value of discipline, power of commitment and depth of conviction. My father, Skip, a loving teacher who took the time to ask me what I thought and allowed me the freedom to express it. To him goes my gratitude for making me believe I could be, do and have anything I wanted. To both my parents I extend my gratitude for their example, for after 20 years of being divorced, they decided to get out of their ruts, set aside the past and continue their lives in a state of love. They remarried in 1984. Hooray for them!

To Uncle Paul go my thanks for showing me how to create and be aware of the "magical" moments in life and to share that with others. Aunt Jackie and Uncle Johnny taught me how to play, be rowdy and have a great time. Thank you for that.

I must now give a very special thank-you to the woman who taught me what true unselfish love is all about. The lady in my life who is the epitome of what it means to give—my dear sweet grandmother, the late Bertha Carpenter.

To all the other family members and loved ones who have touched my life, I say thank you. Without you, my life wouldn't be as rich as it is today.

Life would move at a much slower pace and it would be much more difficult to achieve our dreams were it not for the mentors who come into our lives to speed along our growth. I've been blessed with two very special mentors to whom I owe a tremendous amount of gratitude: Rex Gamble and Mark Victor Hansen. Rex helped me get started as a professional speaker, and Mark quantum-leaped my experience by being both a friend and a role model that I could follow.

Last, but not least, I want to thank the Mile High Church of Religious Science for giving me a spiritual philosophy by which to live my life. Dr. Fred Vogt and Dr. Roger Teel showed me that "there is a power for good in the Universe that is greater than we are and we can use it."

If it is true that we are a reflection of those around us, I'm very pleased with the picture I see.

—Debra Jones

Introduction

To touch as many lives as I can in a positive way is the goal for my life. I have written this book because I believe there is a wonderful resource wasting away. It is the extraordinary talent of ordinary people.

Each of us has within us something that makes us extraordinary. We all have our own special qualities that set us apart from the masses of humanity. The tragedy is that so many people have convinced themselves that they're not special and, therefore, just existing is okay. Just existing is not okay—*it's blasphemy!*

Socialization teaches us to accept our place in the world and be content. Don't let anyone pigeon-hole you. Don't waste away at a job you hate! Don't stay in relationships that damage your spirit. Find out what you want and then pursue it.

Discovering what makes you happy is what this book is all about. Fasten your seat belts. We're about to take off on a ride toward your dreams.

—*Debra Jones*

Confusion Is the Prelude to Clarity

The lure of the distant and the
difficult is deceptive.
The great opportunity is where you are.

—John Burroughs

It's what you learn after you know it all that counts.

—John Wooden

It's easy for some people to discount the success of others by saying, "It's easy for them. They're so lucky. They haven't had to live through what I've lived through." What they don't see are the fires of the past that forged that person's iron will so that he or she could go on to make great strides in life; and they don't see all the effort that went into rising from the ashes.

If life has taught me nothing else, it has definitely taught me this: Everyone has a story. Some are more colorful and painful than others, but everyone's got one. No one gets to the place at which he or she has arrived without a full spectrum of events occurring in their lives—some good, some not so good. It's what we do with who we are that matters. This story is being told with the hope that it will prove to be helpful to someone who may be traveling a similar path.

The vantage point from which I have written this book is very different from the place where this story began. Today I am the president of a multimillion-dollar mail-order and seminar business. I am married to the man of my dreams and the love of my soul. We have two beautiful children who fill our lives with joy and we live in a wonderful house on a lake where we are surrounded by the beauty of nature every day. It's great now, but it certainly wasn't always this way.

Not long ago my life was filled with massive confusion. I didn't know where I wanted to go or what I wanted to do. All I knew was that my life wasn't working. I didn't know how to fix it. Anyone who's ever been in a circumstance like that knows how lost it can make you feel and how frustrating it is. My frustration began to end with the arrival of a little dark cloud that taught me that confusion is a prelude to clarity. I have found that I'm not alone in having had this struggle. There are a lot of people who don't know what they want. All they know is they don't have it.

Have you ever experienced a time in your life when it seemed there was a little dark cloud that followed you everywhere you went? For some people the situation lasts only a few days, for others a few months, and still others make it their life's work!

My experience with the little dark cloud occurred a number of years ago and, fortunately, lasted only a few months. Prior to those few months you would have said, to look at me, that I was on top of the world. I had graduated from college with top honors, was married to a wonderful man with whom for years I had shared a happy home. I had a great job in the computer industry and, from all indications, my life seemed destined to be nothing short of fabulous. In other words, it appeared that I had learned what I needed to know to make life work. However, nothing could have been further from the truth. Within a matter of months, I systematically destroyed every avenue of life that one would deem valuable. Of course, while it was going on, I didn't think I had anything to do with what was causing those problems. Things were just *happening* to me.

It seemed that no matter what I did or how hard I tried, everything I touched turned into a mess. Although it stayed only a few months, I thought that little dark cloud would never leave.

What I now know, looking back on that experience, is that the string of *bad* things that happened *to* me were nothing more than life trying to give me a message, so that I could learn a vital lesson about balanced living. My life was totally out of balance, but I was too wrapped up in it to see what was going on and the problems I was creating. Some people learn faster than others. I wish I could say I was a quick learner at that time, but I wasn't.

Have you ever noticed that when life is trying to give you a message, it usually sends it in the form of a little problem? If you're a quick learner, that's the end of it. If you're not, life sends you a bigger message in the form of a bigger problem. If you still don't get it, look out—life is about to bring you a full-scale disaster. It wasn't until I was knocked flat on my back that I finally set ego aside and allowed myself to become teachable. Like I said, some people learn faster than others.

The first little "message" that life sent my way was that I massacred a marriage that had meant a great deal to me. Our priorities were out of whack and my husband and I had ended up in competition with each other, which caused us to grow apart. We had stopped putting each other as the focus of our marriage and had instead focused on our occupations. We had become totally self-absorbed in what we were doing. Unfortunately, what we were doing didn't include each other.

Did I think the demise of my marriage had anything to do with me? No, absolutely not. I had been wronged. I did what any good, self-respecting woman would do. I cried buckets and buckets of tears, tried to patch my heart up as best I could and go on with my life. Picture a damsel in distress with her head thrown back in a very dramatic manner and the backside of her hand to her forehead, making absolutely ridiculous statements such as, "I shall never love again!" in a slight Southern drawl. That was the part I was playing. Had I learned anything about balanced living? No.

My antidote for a failed marriage and the pain that comes with it was something I called "rotational dating." Not believing I could find everything I wanted in one man (and keeping myself at a safe distance by not letting anyone get too close to me), I dated one person for sporting events, another for the symphony, another for good conversation, another for romantic dinners at expensive restaurants, etc. I lived fast and played hard. I wouldn't allow myself to feel the pain of my circumstance. Consequently, I didn't learn from it. I ran from it.

Shortly after my marriage had fallen apart, I was promoted to a management position and transferred from Dallas to Denver. It couldn't have come at a better time. I would move and start my life over again with a clean slate. You know the only problem with moving? You take you with you!

I poured my heart and soul into my new job, working as many hours in the course of a day as I possibly could. A few months after arriving in Denver I found that I hated my job, I hated the people I worked with and I hated my life. Had I learned anything about balance? No. So I decided to quit and take off on a 5,000-mile road trip to "find" myself. Five thousand miles later and a lot of money spent, I decided that I had better rejoin the world and get back to work, so I accepted a national sales position with a computer firm in Boulder, Colorado. I said, "I know what I need. I need a fresh start. I know what—I'll move!" So I picked up and moved to Boulder.

Have you ever gone to work for a company that doesn't pay you a lot and so they give you a big title? My title was so big I needed about four business cards to accommodate it. I was traveling all over the country for this firm, selling computer systems. It seemed like things were going fine. What I didn't know was that it was the calm before the storm.

I believe heavily in the reward system and I had had success as a salesperson. So when the Christmas/New Year's holiday rolled around, I decided to give myself a long ski trip to Aspen. Have you ever been skiing in Aspen? If you have, you know you've got to bring more money than you've ever seen printed! Money seems to flow through your hands like water when you're in Aspen.

Well, I had a wonderful time over the holiday season and when I returned home to Boulder, I thought I had better drop by the office to pick up my messages that had accumulated while I'd been away. When I reached the office door, I saw a padlock on it and a note from a bank that read that they had confiscated the contents of the premises. For those of you who have never worked for a company that's gone into bankruptcy, that's what happens. The bank seizes the assets. All my files from years in the computer industry were in that office and I never got them back. I said to myself, "This might not be good."

I went home and opened my mailbox. My last commission check, which was several thousand dollars, had bounced like a rubber ball. My last expense check, which was also several thousand dollars, had also bounced. Now, bear in mind that I had been in Aspen spending money like crazy. This was not a good time to get a bounced check. I looked at those checks and said to myself, "This might not be good."

The president of the firm for which I was working had simply vanished with the cash assets of the business. We had just sold hundreds of thousands of dollars in computer systems to people who had nothing to show for their money. People started calling me at home because I was the only representative of the company they could find. I began talking to myself and wondering, "Can they throw me in jail for this? I was just an employee; I didn't know what was going on." Life was not looking good. Then I got a brilliant idea. I said to myself, "I know what—I'll move!"

So once again I picked up and moved, back to Denver, where the *real* world lived, and I decided to get a *regular* job at a *regular* company and get on with my life. Had I learned my lesson about balance yet? No.

Within a few weeks, I had a number of car accidents. The last one was fairly significant. I was just minding my own business, driving down the street, when all of a sudden a car broadsided me, totaling my car. Fortunately, my seat belt protected me from serious injury.

Have you ever noticed that when things like this are happening to you that you begin to talk to yourself? I had begun saying things to myself like, "What's the deal here? I'm a good person. I don't understand why all this stuff keeps happening to me. I'm just minding my own business and it seems the world is out to get me."

Back to the car accident. I hate to make gross character generalizations about people because there are always exceptions to the rule. However, I would ask that you bear with me on this one. As the other person involved in the accident began walking toward me, I noticed that he was completely covered in tattoos and had no front teeth. I said to myself, "This might not be good."

To make a long story short, he was an escaped convicted felon. They arrested him on the spot and took him to jail. As they were hauling him away, I screamed to them, asking, "Does that man have any insurance?" Needless to say, he didn't.

Here I was beginning a new year. I had no job. I had no love relationship in my life because I had long since run off anyone who tried to care about me. I had no money. In fact, I was very close to what I so delicately refer to as financially embarrassed. And now, I had no means of transportation. My car was a wreck. Did I get the message life was trying to give me? No. Like I said, I wasn't a very fast learner.

The next thing that happened was I got sick. To this day, they're not sure what was wrong with me, but I was terribly ill. Had I learned my lesson? No.

Then came the straw that broke the camel's back. My mother came and stayed with me to help me straighten out my life!

Now, I don't know if, as an adult, your mother has ever come and moved in with you to help you straighten out your life. But, trust me, mine had military action in mind. After she had nursed me back to health and I had convinced her that I was going to be all right, she went home.

One night after she had gone, I woke up in the middle of the night in a panic. I don't know if you've ever been face to face with real panic before, but it's not a pretty sight. I was scared to death and I had awakened in a cold sweat. I was at a point in my life where things should have been working, and they weren't. My life was a mess. I was unhappy and alone. I had creditors hounding me to pay bills and I didn't have any idea where the money was going to come from to satisfy them. There in the middle of the night, in total darkness, I started to cry.

For the first time ever, I didn't stop myself. You see, my solution for pain up to that point in my life had been to avoid it or anesthetize it. If you're hurting, go party. If you're hurting, work harder; it will take your mind off it. If you're hurting, get busier and there won't be time to feel. If something's uncomfortable, ignore it. Avoid it and it will eventually go away. For whatever reason, this time I chose not to ignore the pain, but to feel it.

I cried and I cried, until there just weren't any more tears to be shed. I remember asking, "Who made this mess?" and I recall hearing a voice say, "You did." Strange as it may sound, with that answer came a peacefulness that has stayed with me throughout subsequent years. You see, for the first time, I got the message that life had been trying to give me all along. I got the message that I am responsible for the life that I create. Realizing that I was the only constant in the entire string of circumstances was a big "Aha" for me. I got the message that to be truly happy wasn't about things, it wasn't about corporate position, it wasn't about any of that. It was about balanced living and being satisfied with who I was and knowing that that was enough.

It wasn't until I reached the destination known as "The Pits" that I had become teachable. Ever been to the pits? It's not a great place, is it? At that time, I decided that I would rebuild my life on balanced terms.

To think about rebuilding my life was a real eye-opener for me because I realized I had participated in a number of self-destructive behaviors, many of which were "old tapes" from my childhood replaying themselves. This was a difficult realization for me because I had always taken pride in being an upbeat, positive-mental-attitude kind of person that could handle anything. During that night, however, it had become obvious to me that I had been a person who had read the books, listened to the tapes, gone to the seminars, but only listened and never really heard. When I reached bottom, I decided that there was nowhere else to go but up and I made the commitment to myself that, from that day forward, I would apply the techniques of successful living that I had listened to for years but had never really applied. It also became crystal clear to me that my life is guided.

I'm not going to get into a religious dissertation here because everyone has an individual view regarding spirituality. However, I can say that my life works best when I stop being in charge, and I allow myself to be led by what some would call intuition and others would say is Divine direction.

For a person who's a control fanatic such as I am, relinquishing control is not an easy thing, but it has definitely been worth it. Connecting with the spiritual side of myself and applying to my life the time-tested techniques of successful living enabled me to turn my life around. The skills that I used to create the life of my dreams are the ideas I want to share with you.

Life is much too precious for it to be lived in mediocrity, pain or confusion. I believe the truth about you is that you were destined to have an abundant life filled with health, wealth, love and joy.

I believe, to the core of my being, that what you want, wants you. It's waiting to come into your life just as soon as you ready yourself mentally. The reason I believe this is because I've watched it happen in my life over and over again. Now I want to share these concepts with you, with the hope that you'll create the life you want, instead of settling for what you get.

TWO

Hello in There

Finding Out Who You Are

Many of our fears are
tissue-paper thin, and a single
courageous step would carry us
clear through them.

—Brendan Francis

A man must consider what a rich realm he abdicates when he becomes a conformist.

—Ralph Waldo Emerson

To begin to create the life we want, we must first take a look at the current state of our lives. Who are we? How did we get where we are? Where do we go from here?

As a child with a vivid imagination, the world appeared to me as an untouched canvas just waiting for my impressions. What an amazement there was in tiny simple wonders. Where do butterflies go? How do clouds stay in the sky? Why can't dogs talk? The world of fantasy was real. I used to tell myself, "I can be the greatest person in the world if I want to. . . ." On and on go the playful conversations of a child.

In our childhood minds lie the answers we need in order to live our entire lives in excitement and abundance. Yet one day, while we're not looking (and much to our surprise), in walks conformity and the scene changes.

Running, jumping, laughing, wild abandonment—where does it go? Subtle messages of "rights" and "wrongs" cloud a young mind's eye, narrowing its wide vision to perceive only predetermined views. In the growing-up process we learn to curtail expression. Many of us master this change in ourselves so well that one day we wake up, get out of bed, take a look at ourselves in the mirror and are shocked to realize that we don't recognize the person looking back at us.

Early in my childhood my destiny in life became very clear to me. I've always known that my life would affect hundreds of thousands of people. This is a grand notion, and being such, it has passed through portals of time, space and influence—sometimes twisting, reshaping and hiding it from my view. There were many times when things seemed so dismal and the barriers so steep that it was difficult to see how my life could ever have the kind of impact I had envisioned as a child, but I *never* lost the dream.

Breaking through barriers is what this book is about. Each journey begins with one step, and the sheer act of beginning thrusts you into a world of freedom, creativity, aliveness and expression beyond your most extravagant expectations. The question is not whether you are capable of having what you want, because I know you can. The question is: Are you ready for it?

Many people concern themselves with being normal rather than natural.

—Lee Gibson

Idealism and adventuresome attitudes in our society are thought to be reserved for the wealthy and the young. The rest of us are taught early on that we must work for a living and be practical. For a time in our lives, which is generally during our youth, we are encouraged to explore and embrace all that the world has to offer. Unfortunately for most people, this is the most alive they ever feel. At some point they choose to accept that, from this point forward, life for them will shut down rather than open up—in order that they may fulfill their "responsible" role.

The messages come through loud and clear that it's okay to laugh but don't be too silly. It's okay to be smart but not too smart. It's okay to want more but don't be greedy. It's okay to think but don't question custom. It's okay to win but not all the time. It's okay to love but don't be sexual. It's okay to achieve but don't be different. It's okay to be strong, but not too strong. It's okay to be independent, but don't be a loner. And the big one—it's okay to dream but don't waste time being ridiculous.

Many of us learn that moderation is all we should expect and that to yearn for more is being ungrateful. Watch out! When you start to think that wanting more makes you an ingrate, someone has done a great job of planting seeds of guilt in your mind. Once planted, guilt flourishes. It is up to you to eliminate the guilt you harbor that robs your life of joy and passion.

I have to live for others and not for myself; that's middle-class morality.

—George Bernard Shaw

It's time to realize that you don't have to be mediocre. There is more to life and it is yours for the taking, but first you must muster the courage to peek out of your rut. The simple fact that you are reading this book says that you are ready for some changes.

Mediocrity is something I have always avoided like the plague. For years, I've had a sign on my desk that reads, "I'd rather die than be mediocre." I know that's not a philosophy by which everyone would choose to live. But for me, if mediocrity is the best I can expect out of life, I'd just as soon check out right now because mediocrity isn't exciting to me. I spend more time at my job than any other collective daily activity in which I involve myself. So I absolutely refuse to spend that much of this precious thing we call life in an activity that isn't a passion for me.

Refusing to accept mediocrity is an attitude with a large price tag, but worth every penny.

I've not always been well equipped to choose my own path and direction. As with any growth experience, it has been an evolutionary journey. The journey has made me a student of myself. As I learn more about myself and the planet on which we reside, a Truth becomes more evident to me. The Truth is that everyone deserves to have whatever he or she wants in life as long as it is not hurtful to others.

The wonder of this is that not only do we deserve it, but we are capable of being, doing, having and getting whatever we want—ourselves. It is so simple. All you have to do is listen to yourself and you will have all your answers. The difficulty arises in finding out where our voice resides, since we have muffled it for years by living according to other people's expectations.

---

*I don't know the key to success,
but the key to failure is trying
to please everybody.*

—Bill Cosby

As is true for many people, I started molding myself to live the way I thought others wanted me to at a very young age. As children, we are willing to express ourselves with an uninhibited wild joy and zest for living. Yet soon we realize what others find distasteful, so we change. A certain amount of this is good in that it allows us to function in society. That's not the part that concerns me.

The part I want to explore are the changes we make in ourselves to *please* others, not realizing that those people are never going to be pleased. It's impossible to please someone who isn't pleased with him- or herself.

People who manipulate your actions through guilt to fill gaps in their own lives never feel fulfilled, and you'll probably always feel like you're "coming up short" in your efforts to gain their approval. Consequently, you can feel guilty as you try to assume responsibility for creating someone else's happiness. I should know: I tried doing that for most of my life and it doesn't work.

It wasn't until I could break that cycle that I was able to realize that guilt is one of the largest deterrents keeping people from being who they are and achieving what they want.

Those of us who want a great deal out of life are often ridiculed by others who say, "Well, who are you, Big Shot?" "Too good for us, huh?" "Why can't you just be happy with the way things are?" Why do you always want something more?" "Why can't you just be satisfied and leave well enough alone?"

Consequently, we begin to look at ourselves in terms of what we want and we begin to wonder if there's something wrong with us. There's nothing wrong with you. You're just different. You're not mediocre. In a world filled with mediocrity, the person who is willing to stand up and demand more stands out from the crowd. Extraordinary people often come under attack. They remind those who are mediocre of their own talent going to waste because they didn't have the courage to use it, nor the initiative to make changes.

In order to be irreplaceable one must always be different.

—Coco Chanel

You must learn to accept for yourself that different is wonderful. When you do, the exhilaration you will feel in regard to your life will be boundless. You will be the most powerful you've ever been—and that's exciting. Yet, knowing that different is okay takes some time. It takes coming to terms with old ideas and it often means saying good-bye to old habits, behaviors and, sometimes, friends.

I've always known that I'm different, but I haven't always known how or why or what purpose it served. Being different, I used to put an enormous amount of energy into trying to make myself fit in with everyone else. I wanted to be accepted by my friends and loved ones. But no matter what I tried, as I grew up my differences continued to surface. Looking back now, I'm glad they didn't die out. However, at the time I wasn't so sure.

Have you ever felt like no one really understands who you are and what you need? It seemed to me that most people in the world fit inside a circle and I was on the outside of that circle looking in. It's not to say that I was the shy, quiet type. In fact, just the opposite was true. I was always the popular kid, the super achiever who won awards and had many friends. Outward appearance would have indicated a good, strong, balanced life, but inside I felt misunderstood and on the outside of the circle. Something about me felt very different.

I felt, as you may have, that there must surely be others who were like me on the outside of the circle. I just didn't know who or where they were, so I continued to try to conform and be who I thought I was "supposed" to be.

Anthony Robbins writes in his wonderful book, *Awaken The Giant Within,* that there are only two motivators in life—pain and pleasure. The pain of living for others got so intense one day that I got fed up with it and decided to quit trying to please everyone else and just be myself.

Once that decision was made, a large group of new friends came into my life who weren't "needy," and I began to see that two opposing thoughts can't occupy the same mind. In other words, I couldn't hang onto the idea that I was living to please others and expect that, at the same time, healthy, non-dependent relationships would flourish in my life. One action was canceling out the possibility of the other occurring. You can't move forward until you let go of the past.

Having done so, life is more wonderful now than I ever dreamed. A lesson I learned, however, is that there is a price to pay. To truly feel alive you must first step out of your rut and have the courage to say, "I'm going for my dreams even if I don't know all the steps I need to take yet. I'm starting anyway because

I do know, at least, what the first step is and I'm taking a risk."

Then (here's the important part) *you must never look back*. You will have just opened the door to a new way of living. That door must be opened by you before the things you want can come into your life. The funny thing is that what you want is waiting for you now and always has been. The only catch is it can't come rushing in until you've set the stage for its arrival.

If you're ready, let's accept some basic premises about who we are and how we got that way, so we can go on and move forward. Let's assume that all of us have a considerable amount of trash in our lives as a result of our childhoods. Let's also assume that we don't have to be victims of that trash for the rest of our lives. The freedom of change lies within the realm of your power. By conquering rut after rut, your power increases and the "boogeyman" of childhood fades away.

Food for Thought

Take a moment to write down five self-limiting beliefs that are a carry-over from your childhood that you would like to banish from your life because they no longer serve you.

1. ______________________________

2. ______________________________

3. ______________________________

4. ______________________________

5. ______________________________

THREE

Dreams Are the Stuff from Which Reality Is Made

We must never try to escape the obligation of living at our best.

—Janet Erskine Stuart

I had an ambition not only to go farther than any man had ever been before, but as far as it was possible for a man to go.

—Capt. James Cook

One of the greatest achievements in life would be if someone were to ask you, “If you could be doing anything in the world that you’d like to be doing, what would it be?” and you were able to answer, “What I’m doing now.” Wouldn’t that be wonderful?

Today I am living the fulfillment of one of my dreams. I am a nationally recognized speaker, I travel extensively to beautiful destinations throughout the country for my clients’ conventions, they pick up all my expenses and I work on my terms. I work when I want to and I stay home when I want to.

I began dreaming this dream when I was broke and no one wanted to hear anything I had to say. Some would have said that the dream of being a well-known, well-paid speaker based on my circumstances would have been too far-fetched. I totally disagree.

It's been my experience that you're not given a dream unless you've also been given the ability to make it real. Now, of course, that doesn't mean it's going to happen overnight, nor does it mean it's going to be easy. It also doesn't mean you'll make all your dreams turn into reality, but it does mean that you *could* if you wanted it badly enough.

So . . . what are the dreams and aspirations you have for your life? Too many people have forgotten how to dream. Or they've abandoned dreaming in exchange for earning a living. It's time to start to dream again.

Looking back at the great people of history, such as Capt. James Cook, quoted at the beginning of this chapter, it becomes evident to us that great accomplishments were made by great dreamers. These people often appeared to be overnight successes. On closer examination, their lives show not only vision but also a plan for bringing their vision into reality. Deep within the recesses of our minds lie our hopes and dreams. We often deny their existence to ourselves and to others, but if we will allow ourselves the privilege of fantasy and imagination, those dreams will surface readily and spring back to life.

We live in a society that shuns its dreamers. They are chalked off as frivolous, idle, drifters, time wasters, odd, etc. But where would we be without our dreamers? None of the great inventions would have ever been made—if no one had a dream. Plagues would still be ravaging our populations—if no one dreamed of finding a cure. Businesses would not be operating and our entire system of living would collapse—without dreams. So you see, dreams and dreamers are very important.

The pity is that, for the most part, only famous dreamers are applauded and encouraged. It would appear that what brings a dreamer power in this world are success and recognition. Suddenly they seem to make dreaming okay. Most other people, however, are encouraged to conform, to work at their jobs and not waste time daydreaming. The dialogue goes something like this: "After all, let's be realistic. What great things can you expect to achieve with your life, anyway? Right?" My answer to that is a resounding "**WRONG!**"

I've stopped letting people convince me to cancel my dreams. An incredible thing has happened as a result of that decision. I'm accomplishing more of them, and so can you. All you have to do is be willing to take a risk. The first risk is always the most difficult, but after a while you get used to taking risks and they get easier.

Every time an artist dies,
part of the vision of mankind
passes with him.

—Franklin D. Roosevelt

Isn't this true of dreamers as well? Each time we allow ourselves to be beaten down just as our spirit is beginning to soar, we lose something, and so does humanity. Here is a guidepost I have learned to live by over the years. When I have a dream burning inside me and I share that dream with someone and that person says, "Are you crazy?" I know I'm on the right track. People's criticism used to bother me. Now it encourages me because I have found the big prizes in life don't go to those who follow the herd, but to those who blaze their own trail.

Unfortunately, too many people allow their dreams and their creativity to be extinguished by others. I'm reminded of a song by the late Harry Chapin. He describes a wonderfully curious, happy child, with bright dancing eyes, who arrives in art class ready to express the beauty of nature as he sees it. When he is asked to paint flowers, he chooses to use all the colors of the rainbow in all their wonder and glory. However, this doesn't suit the teacher's lesson plan and she reprimands him, saying that the colors of flowers and leaves should always be painted as they appear in nature—with red flowers and green leaves. There's no need to see them otherwise. To this the child replies that nature is full of glorious colors and he sees them all. The teacher sees him as a discipline problem and increases the severity of treatment by isolating him. Our creative young man gets lonely and decides to conform.

Sometimes that's a tough mold to break. One day the young man moves to a new school. The art teacher is enthusiastically encouraging the children to explore with color as they paint their pictures of gardens. When she asks our young man to experiment with some other colors and be creative, he looks at her with an expressionless face and says in a mono tone voice, that the colors of flowers and leaves should always be painted as they appear in nature—with red flowers and green leaves. There's no need to see them otherwise. When I first heard this song it made me want to cry—and it still does.

It's painful when we stop to consider the exploration and creativity that have been squelched along the way. Sometimes it hurts so much to think about what we might have been that we prefer to numb ourselves by saying it doesn't matter. We cop out on ourselves by claiming other priorities had to take over and assume greater importance. I have lived that way in my past and I can tell you that it's no way to live. When you numb yourself to your heartfelt desires, something else moves in and takes its place. It may start as a numb feeling but then it grows into resentment and anger. You may end up hating the person you loved so much that you decided to put your own dreams on hold.

I say nothing is as important as you and your dreams. Until you can love and fully experience yourself, you can't share yourself fully with anyone else.

Over and over again in my travels, women in my audience will come up to me with a pained look of sincere questioning on their face and ask, "How do you do it? How do you manage to run a successful business, be married, have two small children and keep it all together?" When I tell them how it's done, which for me, is hiring help for all the day-to-day mechanics of running a household that I don't care to do so that I can spend more time with my family, they instantly begin to make excuses why that can't work for them.

What they don't choose to see is that I made the decision to hire that help when I didn't have the money to make the dream real. If you wait until everything's perfect before you launch out on faith, you'll never go anywhere.

Here's the bottom line. Until you've got the dream firmly implanted in your mind, your solutions aren't going to start to show up because you're not motivated enough yet to make things happen. You see, dreams don't just waltz right in your front door while you're lounging on the couch waiting for them. You have to go out there and get them. It's amazing. When you get to work, so does the Universe. It gets to work bringing you what you want when you show that you're serious about having it.

If you get nothing else out of this book, hear this: YOU MUST TAKE CARE OF YOURSELF FIRST. YOU CANNOT LIVE *FOR* SOMEONE ELSE OR *THROUGH* SOMEONE ELSE. Don't let anyone take the color out of your rainbow. There are so many colors in the rainbow and the world needs every one.

The most wonderful thing about us as human beings is that as long as we are still alive and lucid, we are capable of making choices. So what if you've been downtrodden? So what if your father's a drunk? So what if you've been abused? So what if you're poor? So what if you're uneducated? So what if your business went bankrupt? So what if you've failed at love before? So what if you're unemployed? You can still choose to be whatever you want and have the kind of life you want. Fortunately, we live in a country that allows that.

The annals of history are full of people who have overcome all obstacles in their way to rise to the pinnacle of greatness. And so can you! Open up the cage that has imprisoned your mind and let it fly. Allow yourself to express and experience the freedom that comes from knowing you can be, do and have whatever you want. If you fall down and fail, that's okay. It's not the end of the world. As long as you're still breathing, you've still got tomorrow to go after it again.

I'm from Oklahoma, and my father used to say to me when I was growing up, "Punkin', there isn't anything so bad that we can't hit the ground rollin', brush ourselves off, and keep on running'. So don't sweat the small stuff." Deep within every fiber of my body I believe this to be so. It's up to you whether you let someone kill your dream. Now, what's your choice? Are you going to give up and be a puppet, and/or a martyr, for others all your life, *or* are you going to go for what you want? After all, if you're living for someone else, you're not really living your life anyway. So what do you have to lose?

Remember, you can always hit the ground rollin', brush yourself off, and keep on running'. Don't sweat the small stuff and, in the overall scheme of things, it's *all* small stuff!

A dream grants what one covets when awake.

—German proverb

You may find that re-acquainting yourself with your dreams requires a little practice—particularly if you've been living comfortably in a rut for a number of years. Ruts can be quite powerful, and yet ruts are nothing more than habits. Strangely enough, we often have a strong affection for our position within those ruts, even if it's unpleasant for us. It was Goethe who said, "Habit is a man's sole comfort. We dislike doing without even unpleasant things to which we have become accustomed." Unfortunately, that is often true. But remember you have a choice, and you can choose now to get out of that rut.

It may seem at first that you don't have any dreams—and that's okay. After all, any skill that we don't exercise and use will have a tendency to get rusty. However, there is a very quick way to clear up that confusion. I'd like to ask you to take a little mental journey with me.

Picture yourself on a large tropical island walking along a white sandy beach. As you look toward the sky, it appears as though it is an infinite film of blue continuing on forever, with pure white puffs of clouds occasionally floating by. The sun warms your skin as you walk, and you feel happy as the tide washes in over your feet and cools them while you move along the beach.

Looking out over the clear turquoise sea, you can see fish and shells several feet down. You're watching the many forms of life in the water when suddenly, you stumble over something and fall. After you brush the sand out of your eyes, you see that you have fallen over a bottle heavily encrusted with jewels. As you look at it more closely, you see that it has a lid. You remove the lid and suddenly you are surrounded with smoke. When the smoke clears, there is a genie standing before you. The genie speaks to you and says, "Thank you for freeing my soul. I want to repay your kindness. I will grant you three wishes for anything you want. What will be your first wish? What do you want more than anything else in the world?"

Write down your first wish.

____

____

____

When you are finished, step up and say, "Hello." You have just been re-introduced to your first dream.

Write down your next two wishes.

____

____

____

____

____

____

There you have it—three dreams. You may be thinking that this sounds a little corny, a little too simplistic. It's okay to be skeptical, but believe me, through this type of vivid imaging, you can have anything you want.

Let's face it—if things were exactly as you wanted them right now, you wouldn't be reading this, would you? Don't sell yourself short. Ask yourself Robert Schuller's well-known question, "How big would you dream if you knew you couldn't fail?" The answer to that question tells you a great deal about what you really want.

Congratulations! Step One has just been completed. You now have some mental pictures of the dreams you would like to have come true in your life. You have also unlocked the door to your creativity and your mental amusement park. Don't be afraid of it. March right in and play to your heart's content. Dreams are not public property unless you choose to make them so. Until then, they are your private domain and are not subject to criticism, so have fun.

Another way to create a great list of dreams is to become aware of the times you say, "I wish . . . so and so" or "If only such and such . . ." and write them down. Some of these items will be of little or no value because you were simply making conversation and didn't really mean what you said. But some of them will excite you to think about their achievement. These may be statements you made out loud, or statements you made to yourself. The "I wish" or "If only" statements you make to yourself are generally very important to you, so make it a habit to increase your awareness of them and write them down. Don't leave out any details.

The more sensorially graphic you make your description of what you want, the easier it will be for you to get it.

When I was rebuilding my life, I began to make a picture book of what I wanted life to be like for me. This may sound strange, but it works. I cut out pictures from magazines that illustrated to me the kinds of images I wanted to have in my own life. I cut out pictures of couples in love, happy families, the kind of home I wanted to live in, the kind of car I wanted to drive, jewelry I liked, places I wanted to visit, etc. I began creating my book 15 years ago and there are only a few things in it that I don't have yet. Notice I said "yet."

I stand in awe of the power of the mind. When you teach your mind what you want, life's circumstances begin to construct themselves in such a way that those things are drawn to you. I believe that thoughts are things and that what you want in your life won't show up until you've first possessed the mental equivalent of it in your mind. In other words, until you've made what you want so real in your mind that you can almost taste and touch it, the likelihood of it showing up in your life is remote. However, once you've made the picture so clear in your mind that all doubt of its accomplishment has been removed, don't be surprised when it appears in your life because it will.

What would life be if we had no courage to attempt anything?

—Vincent Van Gogh

Why does it appear so difficult for us to put energy into our dreams and get them accomplished? I believe the major reason is because we are afraid to take a risk. We are willing to sell ourselves out and settle for a comfortable average living as long as we don't have to experience feelings of anxiety. Many people are so afraid of stepping outside of the norm for themselves that they merely exist. Just existing, just getting by, or just making ends meet is not living. It's survival. Do you want to just survive, or do you want to live? Well, living, my friend—really living—requires some risk. You will, however, find it to be worth the price you pay many times over.

It's all well and good for me to tell you this, but it doesn't give you any answers, does it? To handle risk requires practice, but you must start somewhere to achieve your goals. It has been said that tomorrow is often the busiest day of the week. Don't put off living your life until tomorrow. Tomorrow never gets here and your courage and desire might not be able to hold out waiting for just the right time. You owe it to yourself to begin now.

I am unfaithful to my own possibilities when I await from a change of circumstances what I can do on my own initiative.

—Karl Jaspers

At the ripe old age of five, I began to formally study classical piano. I took to piano like a duck to water, and I became very accomplished at an early age. At the same time, in spite of my ability, there was also a circumstance that created terror in my heart. *Recitals.* Practicing at home I could do just fine. I remembered all the notes, my phrasing was melodious, I played with a great deal of style and expression. All of that seemed to go down the tubes when I stepped onto the stage. My knees turned to water, my fingers to Jell-o. What was holding me back? Fear!

Stepping out onto that stage made me vulnerable, which made me afraid. My fear was based on what I was afraid others would think of me. If I forgot the music, people would think I was stupid. If my technique was sloppy, people would think I was unprepared. If I didn't give a good performance, my teacher would be disappointed in me. If I messed up, I would embarrass my parents and they would be ashamed of me. All of this was ridiculous, of course, but I had allowed it to terrorize me. It was taking the joy out of playing the piano.

At nine years old we have not generally had a lot of experience in dealing with risk. However, at that time, I decided that if I was going to continue as a classical pianist, I was going to have to handle that fear. I started out with small private studio recitals. Prior to the performance, I psyched myself up to know that I was going to play flawlessly and impress the hell out of everyone. Much to my surprise, I did just that! That triumph helped my confidence and I moved on to something bigger—the National Piano Guild competitions.

My goal was to win the award of excellence for outstanding performance. I took the same approach as with the private studio recitals. Before the performance, I psyched myself up to know that I was going to give a wonderful performance. I was still nervous.

The butterflies did not go away, but I kept talking to myself. I continued to tell myself I could do it. That year I won the award of excellence. The fear within me had been beaten. *I had won!* The risk became easier. Not only did I win that year, but I won that award the next seven years in a row! Each year it got to be less of an ordeal—including the last year when I played 15 classical selections (none less than 11 pages long) completely from memory. You see, we really can do whatever we want to when we set our minds to it.

Now, some of you may be reading this and saying to yourself, "That's a nice story about you as a little kid, but what does that have to do with the challenges you face in life as an adult?" Everything. You see, unwavering determination in the pursuit of your dreams is critical whether you're five or 55.

When I decided to go into business for myself, it was not a safe or rational decision. My husband had just started a new business of his own and we had just been married. I didn't have the money to start a business. I had no business plan. I had no collateral with which to go to the bank and get a loan. All I had was a passionate dream to be a professional speaker because I knew my life was to be about impacting the lives of hundreds of thousands of people in a positive way, and it had become obvious to me that being a speaker was how it was going to take place. So I financed my business with credit card debt (which I don't recommend) and I gave myself 90 days to make it. I hit the ground running like crazy. What was my motivation? Fear. I had put everything on the line. I had no choice but to make it. Needless to say, that's called taking a risk, or more aptly put— taking a leap of faith. At the end of every 90 days I made the decision to give myself another 90 days. After I had been self-employed for three years, I finally decided it was going to work. Without being willing to withstand the risk required to give birth to my dream, it would probably still be just a dream rather than the reality I now live every day.

Whatever your dream is, don't let the fear of risk steal it away from you. Start with a small part of your dream and accomplish it. That will give you the courage you need to continue on to the next step. Each step then becomes easier and prepares you for a larger, greater challenge. That is how life changes from surviving to living. And not just living, but living in excitement.

Dealing with and overcoming the fear of risk is only one of the obstacles between most people and the realization of their dreams. So often we find ourselves offering excuses for why we are not doing what we truly want to do. Excuses that kill the dreams (and thus the life) within us range from "I don't have time" to "I'm too old" to "I don't have the money." These excuses are nothing more than your mind's logic and rationale challenging your spirit. It is your justification for why you are denying yourself and your true identity by agreeing to just exist.

An artist's career always begins tomorrow.

—James McNeill Whistler

When we can't seem to muster the energy to do anything else, we can always find the strength to make excuses. I believe an excuse is like a "boogeyman," in that it keeps you from being, doing, and having what you want. The funny thing about this, however, is that once confronted, excuses lose their power. Remember when you were a little kid lying in your room at night in the dark? Suddenly you would hear a noise and then another, and another, and another. The next thing you knew you were convinced that something was in your room, trying to get you. You were scared to death. Your heart was beating a hundred miles an hour. You jumped out of bed and ran faster than you ever ran before to reach the light switch. You flipped on the light and much to your surprise, nothing was there. Calm returned to you in your room. You felt better.

The fears that you have—and the excuses you create to cover up for them—are like terrifying sounds in the night. Confronting those fears and abandoning those excuses is like turning on a light. It will return calmness to you and allow you to go for the accomplishment of your dreams without fear.

Another thing that keeps people from realizing their dreams is procrastination. I give many presentations each year in which I talk with people about getting off dead center and getting on with their lives. Through exposure to thousands of people each year, I have learned a lesson. The degree to which you experience procrastination in your life will be in direct proportion to how undeserving you feel you are to accomplish your dream. By procrastinating, you at least have an excuse for why you didn't get what you said you wanted.

Another trip we lay on ourselves to justify our inactivity is to tell ourselves all the things that are wrong with us. "I'm too old." "I'm too young." "I'm too ugly." "I can't afford it." "I'm too busy." Recognize what you are really saying: You don't believe you can do it; you're incapable. I'm not just saying that you don't believe you can do it because all your circumstances and series of events are working against you. I'm saying you don't really believe you can do it at all— *under any circumstances.* Period! If you find this statement irks you—that's great! This means you still have a chance. So get in there and fight for yourself.

The usual excuse of those who cause others trouble is that they wish them well.

—Vauvenargues

One of the largest stumbling blocks preventing people from being who they know they are is their fear of what other people will think. Is this an obstacle for you? Does it hold you back?

Being in the seminar business enables me to watch the parade of life on a grand scale. I have chosen to make the world my laboratory. Every person I meet, or have an opportunity to observe, teaches me a lesson. That person becomes my subject to study and analyze. In looking at the power of influence that others use on us, I have learned a couple of wonderful lessons. First, if someone is telling me I "ought/should" do something or I "ought/should" behave in a certain way, that person is manipulating me. Generally this manipulation is helping people to fill a void or satisfy a need in their own life, but they're using me to do it. In the animal kingdom we would call that a parasitic relationship. As we all know, parasites eventually kill their subject or at least weaken them considerably. This doesn't sound like a pretty picture, does it? Yet if you're allowing your life to be dictated by the whims and influence of another person, you're agreeing to have the life drained right out of you.

The second lesson I have learned is a very short one. Anytime I hear someone say, "I'm telling you this for your own good," I don't listen because generally *it isn't.*

Half the failures in life arise
from pulling in one's horse
as he is leaping.

—J.C. and A.W. Hare

Dreamers and their dreams—they are what make our world worthwhile. It's what separates us from the beasts of the field and the race of the survival of the fittest. We've looked at a lot of things that could be holding you back. The question you must ask yourself now is: Are you ready to realize your dreams? I believe you are on the brink of creating something wonderful in your life. Something inside you is crying to break out and be free, or you wouldn't be reading a book like this. Believe in yourself. You are the best "you" you will ever have.

Sure, you may encounter some risks, but as Bob Trask says in his tapes, *Winning All the Time*, "You must risk in order to win." Let yourself win and tell the world to look out. Give up the chains that have held you down. You are like a helium balloon. All you have to do is cut the cord and YOU WILL FLY!

Food for Thought

Dreams are important to have in all areas of your life. Take a moment to complete the questions below. If you find that you don't have an immediate answer for some, that's okay. A lot of people don't have their dreams clarified. In the next chapter, you'll learn to crystallize your dreams, moving them from the abstract to the concrete. Complete as many of these questions as you can. You can go back and fill in the others later.

Dream Weaving

1. Do you have the job of your dreams? ____ yes ____ no

   If you answered "no," what would the job of your dreams be like?

   ____

   ____

   ____

   ____

2. Do you currently have a loving, intimate relationship in your life that supports you in your growth? ____ yes ____ no

   If you answered "no," take a moment and describe your dream relationship in as much detail as possible.

   ____

   ____

   ____

   ____

3. Do you have the kind of friendships that you would like to have in your life?
____ yes ____ no

Describe your ideal best friend.

____

____

____

____

4. Do you have nurturing relationships with all your family members? ____ yes ____ no

Which ones need to be improved?

____

____

What needs to change to make them better?

____

____

5. Are you comfortable financially?
____ yes ____ no

What would you need to be financially secure?

____

____

6. Are you living the kind of lifestyle that makes you happy? ____ yes ____ no

If money were no object and you could have anything you wanted, what kind of lifestyle would you be living?

____

____

____

____

7. Do you have health challenges?
____ yes ____ no

If you answered "yes," what would your perfect health condition be?

____

____

____

____

8. Are you happy? ____ yes ____ no

What changes would be required to make you happy?

____

____

____

____

9. What "wild and crazy" thing have you always wanted to do, but felt you couldn't?

____

____

____

____

What prevents you from doing that?

____

____

____

____

At the Fork in the Road?

Clarifying What You Want

It does not take much strength to
do things, but it requires great strength
to decide on what to do.

—Elbert Hubbard

If we are ever in doubt about what to do, it is a good rule to ask ourselves what we shall wish on the morrow that we had done.

—Sir John Lubbock

If you had some difficulty completing all the questions from the previous chapter, don't worry about it. Remember, confusion is the prelude to clarity. It has been my experience that when I'm the most confused, I'm the closest to getting my answer. Oftentimes it isn't until we are thoroughly confused about our life, and what we want to make of it, that the answer suddenly pops out at us. I believe this happens because some of us are so control-oriented that if we're not experiencing confusion, we're not open to suggestion.

Many, many people have a hard time quantifying what it is that they want. In fact, you may find that even when you get a crystal clear picture of what you want, you're not finished. Why? As you grow and change, so does the picture of what you want in your life. So it's always an evolutionary process.

There are, however, some things you can do to provide yourself with greater direction so that you improve your odds of accomplishing your dreams. Accomplishing your dreams is important because from what I understand, one time through *this* life is all we get. Don't put your dreams on hold for so long that you miss your chance to experience them.

We are all too familiar with the tragic scenario of the old lady dying unfulfilled in the county nursing home. She spent her life on her knees as a maid scrubbing floors, scratching out a living in the county courthouse for 30 years. On her deathbed she experiences an opportunity to reflect on her life. She regrets that she did not pursue her talents as a dancer. Now her legs will never dance—sad but true. After our lives are spent, there is no way to rewind the clock to give ourselves a chance to do what we really wanted to do.

Now is the only chance we have. This sounds simplistic, but are you really taking advantage of it?

Do not sell your life for a few dollars, security and a gold watch at retirement. Life is too precious. It is blasphemy to consider not pursuing the talents you have. It was Kahlil Gibran who said, "They deem me mad because I will not sell my days for gold; and I deem them mad because they think my days have a price." Your days are indeed priceless, so you must decide what you want to do with them.

I have always believed I was a very goal-directed person, living life toward a certain end. However, I found that when confronted with the question of what did I really want to do with my life, I didn't have any answers. I only had generalities, and generalities won't get you there. That's like being in Colorado, asking for directions to Tulsa, Oklahoma, and getting a response like, "Well, it's between Kansas and Texas." As the old saying goes, "Close only counts in horseshoes." In life it doesn't get you much except missed opportunities.

Sure, in looking at my life I could give you a general idea of what I wanted to do with my career and my personal relationships, but it had more to do with supporting status quo than with what I *really* wanted to do. I had no specific plans for getting what I wanted because I'd never really sat down and spelled out in concrete terms, "This is what I want." Have you? Most people haven't.

I suppose one of the reasons for this is that, these days, it seems everyone's so busy. See if this scene sounds familiar:

You wake up in the morning after having hit the snooze alarm one too many times. You look at the clock and begin your day in a state of total panic. Oh my gosh, you're LATE! You jump out of bed and go tearing around the house at record speed. You snatch the children out of their beds, dress them before they've hardly had a chance to open their eyes, pop some "instant" breakfast into their mouths and scoot them out the door in the nick of time so that they can catch the bus and not be late for school. You jump into your car and go screaming down the highway. Of course, as usual, some idiot has fallen asleep at the traffic light while you're hyperventilating in the car behind them. You finally make it to the office. You work like a dog all day long. When you get off work, you go rushing to pick up the kids and get to their athletic events, dance or music lessons, etc. You get home in time to fix a quick dinner, which various family members eat at different times. You watch a little TV, maybe read the paper, maybe work out a little bit and then fall into your bed, where you instantly fall into a coma because you're so tired. Then, before you know it, the alarm clock goes off and you do it all again. We call this *life!* Does this sound familiar? Is it any wonder that you may not have taken the time to decide what you want to do with your life? It certainly wouldn't surprise me if you've never given it a moment's thought.

Not taking time to care for ourselves is why we have a world full of apathetic participants. They're going through the motions. There's no fire in people's lives because they're living someone else's dream or playing someone else's part.

When I realized that I was living my life without knowing what I wanted, it became simultaneously evident to me that I was existing and not living. That thought frightened me. I realized that to waste a moment meant I had lost it forever. It could not be recaptured or re-created. It was gone. I knew I couldn't bear to reflect on my life in my later years and say, "I wish I'd done so-and-so." That would break my heart. So, I decided to change my course. If you have not made a commitment to yourself about what you want to do with your life, perhaps the following ideas will help you.

Doubt of any kind cannot be resolved except by action.

—Thomas Carlyle

My first priority was to determine what I really wanted to do. It's easy to do what we think we "should" do or what others "want" us to do. But until you are honest with yourself about what *you* want to do, you will not feel excited about living your life. You will feel oppressed, and this often turns into depression. Depending on its severity, this can become life-threatening. It may kill you quickly through suicide, or slowly through a wasted life.

So, how do you decide what to do? The best place to start is to ask yourself, "What do I want to say I've done at the end of my life?"

Make a list and write down everything that comes to mind. Let the ideas flow. Don't be judgmental. List them all.

Life's Accomplishments

____

____

____

____

____

____

____

____

____

____

____

____

Imagine that there are no restrictions on you. You can have anything your heart desires and you can do anything you want. There are no obstacles. Make a list of 25 things you would do if this were true.

Do It Now

1. ____
2. ____
3. ____
4. ____
5. ____
6. ____
7. ____
8. ____
9. ____
10. ____
11. ____
12. ____
13. ____
14. ____
15. ____
16. ____

17. ______________________________
18. ______________________________
19. ______________________________
20. ______________________________
21. ______________________________
22. ______________________________
23. ______________________________
24. ______________________________
25. ______________________________

In finding out what we want to do with our lives, it's important to discover what truly interests us, excites us and brings us joy. Here's the reason—when you're doing what you love, you tend to succeed more easily. You see, life wasn't meant to be about struggle. We create struggle.

List 100 items that you are interested in, find exciting and stimulating. It may take several attempts to complete this list because you may not be accustomed to the thought of living with that much abundance in your life. Consequently, it may be a challenge for you to come up with 100 things that interest you and bring you joy. It's okay if it takes you days or even weeks to complete this list. Keep this book nearby. Whenever something pops into your head that you really enjoy, grab the book, turn to these pages and write it down.

Begin It Now

List 100 items, activities, etc. that interest you and bring you joy.

1. ______________________________
2. ______________________________
3. ______________________________
4. ______________________________
5. ______________________________
6. ______________________________
7. ______________________________
8. ______________________________
9. ______________________________
10. ______________________________
11. ______________________________
12. ______________________________
13. ______________________________
14. ______________________________
15. ______________________________
16. ______________________________
17. ______________________________
18. ______________________________
19. ______________________________
20. ______________________________
21. ______________________________
22. ______________________________
23. ______________________________
24. ______________________________
25. ______________________________
26. ______________________________

27. ______________________________
28. ______________________________
29. ______________________________
30. ______________________________
31. ______________________________
32. ______________________________
33. ______________________________
34. ______________________________
35. ______________________________
36. ______________________________
37. ______________________________
38. ______________________________
39. ______________________________
40. ______________________________
41. ______________________________
42. ______________________________
43. ______________________________
44. ______________________________
45. ______________________________
46. ______________________________
47. ______________________________
48. ______________________________
49. ______________________________
50. ______________________________
51. ______________________________
52. ______________________________

53. ______________________________
54. ______________________________
55. ______________________________
56. ______________________________
57. ______________________________
58. ______________________________
59. ______________________________
60. ______________________________
61. ______________________________
62. ______________________________
63. ______________________________
64. ______________________________
65. ______________________________
66. ______________________________
67. ______________________________
68. ______________________________
69. ______________________________
70. ______________________________
71. ______________________________
72. ______________________________
73. ______________________________
74. ______________________________
75. ______________________________
76. ______________________________
77. ______________________________
78. ______________________________

79. ________________________
80. ________________________
81. ________________________
82. ________________________
83. ________________________
84. ________________________
85. ________________________
86. ________________________
87. ________________________
88. ________________________
89. ________________________
90. ________________________
91. ________________________
92. ________________________
93. ________________________
94. ________________________
95. ________________________
96. ________________________
97. ________________________
98. ________________________
99. ________________________
100. ________________________

When your list is complete, go back and give each item some additional thought.

If your interests are career-oriented, find at least three to five ways that you could make money pursuing that interest. Do this with each of your 100 items.

You will find that some items excite you more than others and ideas will flood your page as you write. These are the items that you should pursue further. With these, you have the inner resources necessary to bring that desire into your reality. You have the power to make these things happen right now. You are ready for them. Your creativity is just waiting to be unleashed to support you in the achievement of those desires.

If your interests are relationship-oriented or philanthropic in scope, use the same process, but tailor the additional thought to support those directions. For example, if you want a loving relationship in your life, start first by listing the qualities you would want that person to have (refer back to the exercise you did at the end of Chapter 3). Then ask yourself, "Do I have those qualities"? If the answer is "No," make a plan for how you can cultivate these qualities. Do that with each item on your list.

This is important because in the balance of life, there is a natural law always in effect. That law says, "Like attracts like." Remember that old cliché, "Birds of a feather flock together?" There's a lot of truth in that saying. It means that the people, things, events and circumstances that we have in our lives are mirror representations of ourselves. Therefore, if we're seeking changes, we must start by changing ourselves and our perceptions. Get the idea?

After you have compiled your three lists, look at them all together. By looking at the lists side by side, you will begin to see some common threads running through the lists. These are the things you should pursue. Sometimes people believe they can do this in their mind without writing it down. Trust me, you can't. Have you ever tried comparing 300 to 500 items mentally? If you can do that, Einstein should have taken lessons from you.

Another benefit of writing down this information is that it allows you to take an objective look at what you want to do. The whole purpose of this activity is to get your mind off of blocks and obstacles and focus it on solutions.

For him who has no concentration, there is no tranquility.

—Bhagavad Gita

From your list, you want to formulate a plan for how you can accomplish your dream, step by step. Select the three most important dreams you want to accomplish and begin. The easiest way to do this is to start at the end result and work your way backward. Let me show you what I mean.

Remember I said that I've known all my life that what I did with my life was going to affect hundreds of thousands of people. When I got specific with myself in determining what I really wanted to do, writing a book was one of the action steps I chose to help me in accomplishing my dream. Starting at the end result, I selected the day I wanted the book to hit the marketplace. I questioned the publisher regarding the lead time necessary from the time the copy was submitted to the publisher until it was delivered to the shelves in the store. The outline of the chapters was the next crucial step. How many chapters did I want to have? How many pages did I want to average per chapter? By focusing on these details, I soon knew how many chapters I had to complete per week and how many pages I had to write per day. By sticking to this schedule the book was very easy to write. However, a year before I would have considered writing a book an impossible task. You see, a year ago, I was looking at the problem and not the steps to the solution.

The message I'm trying to get to you is that you can be, do and have anything you want. The trick is to accomplish it in bite-size portions. The only thing keeping you from what you want is fear. That fear gains power when you look at your situation in one lump sum. It appears the attainment of our dreams is impossible because we see our dreams far off in the distance—something out of our reach. If someone set a watermelon down in front of you and said, "Eat this whole thing," you would be hard-pressed to gobble it up in one bite. However, by taking your time and eating it bite by bite, you could soon devour the whole thing. The accomplishment of your dreams can work the same way.

Let the power of planning work for you. You will be amazed at how powerful, exhilarated and confident you will feel. The best way I know of to rid your life of boredom and the feeling of mediocrity is to complete one step toward the achievement of your dream each and every day. It doesn't matter how small that step is. Each completion will empower you. It's great fun, too, because your friends and loved ones will be so amazed by your strides. They'll view it as an overnight accomplishment. Accept the praise and smile warmly, knowing that for quite some time you've been conducting your own personal revolution.

One half of knowing what you want is knowing what you must give up before you get it.

—Sidney Howard

One of the first things you will have to give up in order to get what you want is indecision. Working through the lists we just discussed will give you some clarity regarding the direction you should take. Some people still have a difficult time seeing their path clearly, in spite of all the analyzing, list-making and logic. When I find that happening to me, I listen to my little voice within. Some people refer to it as intuition. I should know by now to listen to it first because it's always right. Yet, for some reason, I can't seem to get my ego out of the way, which says, "I can figure this out for myself—logically." This often causes me to take a longer route to where I want to be.

The easiest way I know to determine if you are on the right path or not is to take a reading on your feelings and the events occurring in your life. Let's say that you are pursuing the first three dreams from your list and you are giving each of them your best effort. You will find that one direction works better than the others. Things seem to be easier to accomplish, etc. You can almost bet that this dream is fulfilling your purpose. You are doing what you're supposed to be doing in this life by following this path. I don't want to get into a real spiritual discussion of this; however, there are forces in the Universe that guide us toward our greater good. The key is that we must become aware of the guideposts outlining our paths.

When you make a decision to pursue a dream and you give it your best effort, it will come to you easily—if it is fulfilling your purpose. However, if you are pursuing a dream with your best effort, and every turn you make creates another problem for you, chances are that isn't a dream you should be pursuing. Those are the guideposts the Universe provides for you.

You'll notice I said giving it your best effort. I'm not talking about using the first little difficulty as an excuse to quit. What I'm referring to means that you have tried everything, you've given it your best shot and it's *still* not working. This, then, is a guidepost saying, "No, I don't think you should go this way. There's something else you're supposed to do." The more practice you have with using your intuition and your "gut feel," the more you will become aware of these guideposts and make life easier on yourself. You just have to learn to get out of your own way.

Fear is static that prevents me from hearing my intuition.

—Hugh Prather

In spite of the fact that you have diligently prepared your lists and made concrete plans, you may still be confronted with fear from time to time. When I'm just about to "make it," fear jumps in to make one last valiant effort to keep me in my rut.

Fear is not unlike a dictator trying to crush a revolution of people striving for freedom. The more the people fight for their cause, the stronger the forces of the dictator must become to try to suppress their spirit. Freedom, however, is a strong fire not easily extinguished. Just try to remember that as you are making up excuses and reasons for why you should quit, why you can't make it, or why it's not worth it, that fear is gaining on you. At that moment it knows more than you do that you are just about to succeed and accomplish your dream. Don't give up. You are knocking on the door of success. Learn to listen to your intuition, not circumstance.

Fear will be the strongest when you are the closest to winning, and it won't die easily. It knows that if you win, it will perish, so it will put up quite a fight.

There is nothing better than the encouragement of a good friend.

—Katherine Buler Hathaway

To speed your growth and development, one of the questions you may want to ask yourself is, "Am I the biggest hotshot in my circle of friends?" If the answer to that is "yes," you need some new friends! I'm not being facetious when I say that. I'm serious.

If you're the biggest hotshot in your circle of friends, you're not growing. You're having to pull everyone else along. To take a quantum leap toward the achievement of your dreams, you need the influence of friends who are farther down the path than you are. They will stretch your thinking. They will cause you to grow. They will pull you along, and they won't tolerate your whining.

Let me give you a personal example. One of my longtime friends and mentors is Mark Victor Hansen. Mark is known around the world as a business motivator. He speaks to hundreds of thousands of people a year. He has written many books and is a coauthor of *The New York Times* bestseller, *Chicken Soup for the Soul.*

Many years ago when my life had hit rock bottom and I had personally destroyed every avenue of life that one would deem valuable, I *happened* to attend one of Mark's seminars. I had heard him speak before, but on this particular day, I really *heard* what he had to say. There is a saying: "When the student is ready, the teacher will appear." I was ready and there he was! He spoke at length about the power of goal-setting and visualization as a fast track to accomplishing your dreams. I purchased his book, *Future Diary,* which is a guide for mapping out your life, and in it I wrote that I wanted Mark Victor Hansen as a personal friend of mine.

This might not sound like a big deal to you, but you've got to put this into the proper context. At that time, Mark was a millionaire businessman. I was on the verge of bankruptcy. He was a famous speaker.

No one knew who I was. He lived in Southern California. I lived in Denver. The odds of our paths crossing or our social circles mixing were a million to one. That didn't matter to me. I wrote in my book anyway that I wanted Mark Victor Hansen as a personal friend of mine.

Within a matter of a few months, circumstances began arising that enabled our paths to cross. We began a friendship that has now lasted many years. Our children are the same ages and have enjoyed playing with each other on the ski slopes of Aspen, where it was my pleasure to have Mark and his family as my guests. We have enjoyed some of the wonderful beaches of the world, traveled to terrific resorts and experienced many, many good times together.

Here's the key. You don't have to know how things are going to work out. All you have to do is embrace the vision and take the first step. If you hold the vision with unwavering determination, life will work out the circumstances. You must remember—what you want, wants you.

Closely tied to this is one of the most valuable lessons I have learned in my life. It relates to the Master Mind concept outlined in Napoleon Hill's book, *Think and Grow Rich.* This concept deals with sharing your ideas with one or more persons on a regular basis to get their input and suggestions regarding what you're doing with your dreams. It's important to be very selective when choosing the members of your group. You must respect their opinions. It is wise to select individuals whom you feel are of equal or greater competence than yourself. The whole idea behind this is for people to assist each other in achieving their goals. It's the epitome of "Two heads are better than one."

The concept works like this. Seek out individuals whom you like, respect and admire. Tell these people you would like to get together with them periodically to discuss your goals and your progress toward achieving them. Tell them you would appreciate their input regarding ways to improve your performance. The concept works best when it is mutually beneficial. Chances are, these people will be working on some area of their life in which they would welcome your support and suggestions as well. When you find a match like this, you have the beginnings of what could be the greatest impetus to accomplishing your goals rapidly.

There are two people with whom I meet regularly to discuss what's going on in my life as I proceed with accomplishing my dreams. I respect these people and value their opinions. When I tell them I'm going to do something, it carries more weight than just saying it to myself. The reason for this is not only that I respect these individuals, but I want them to respect me as well. I value the time they spend with me. Each is a very busy professional person, and as such, I wouldn't think of wasting their time by discussing empty plans with them.

This extra bit of outside pressure creates a standard for me to live up to. No one puts that pressure on me except me, but it has proved to be the extra nudge I need to assist me in actually accomplishing my goals, rather than just talking about them. If you tell everyone you're going to do something, you can't afford to back down. Your ego won't let you, and consequently you get things done.

Another wonderful thing about a Master Mind group is the brainstorming that takes place. When two minds are joined together, a third mind is created. Oftentimes this third mind is more creative and objective than the other two could ever hope to be individually. When you encounter a situation to which you cannot see a solution, take it to your Master Mind group. It may surprise you at how quickly the solution surfaces through discussion. Having someone to share your difficulties with allows the solution to come to you because you have taken yourself out of the place where you couldn't see the forest for the trees.

Not only does this super mind that gets created with your Master Mind group assist you in business matters, it can also prove to be of enormous assistance in your personal life as well.

I experienced a graphic demonstration of this when I was pregnant with my daughter, Joy, who was our first child. Throughout the pregnancy, Doug and I had done our mental work on the kind of pregnancy we wanted to have and how our darling baby would be incorporated into our life. (For anyone who's pregnant, I highly recommend the book, *The Secret Life of the Unborn Child,* by Thomas Verny and John Kelly.)

Every night just prior to going to sleep, Doug would talk to Joy while she was in my womb. He would say things to her like, "Hi Baby Jones, this is Daddy. We are so excited for you to come and live with us. We're getting ready to go to bed now and I just wanted to let you know that we sleep during the night and we're awake during the day. Good night. We love you."

Having known many friends whose children did not sleep during the night and witnessed the effect that exhaustion had on their lives, we knew we had to help Baby Jones get on our schedule. Within seven days of Joy's birth she began to sleep throughout the night. Coincidence? I don't think so.

Pardon the diversion. Now, back to the Master Mind group.

Although we had prepared for our pregnancy, a situation arose the night I entered the hospital to deliver Joy that caused us to lose sight of our goal for a safe and wonderful delivery. In other words, we became so involved in our problem that we couldn't see a solution.

It seemed I was one of those mothers whose body didn't want to go into labor. I was two weeks past Joy's due date and there was no sign of labor beginning to start. During the last visit to my doctor, I was given a stress test, which indicated that much of the water in the womb was gone (my water had not broken) and Joy was no longer being cushioned by the remaining fluid. I entered the hospital and labor was induced.

We didn't expect the situation caused by inducing labor when there was insufficient fluid to cushion the baby. After several hours, we didn't seem to be getting anywhere. Doug and I had been in the birthing room alone for a while, with the exception of several occasions when a nurse would come in to check on us. All of a sudden, we looked up and found that there were about eight nurses and doctors in the room with us. Joy's movements had set off monitors at a nurses' station and we had an emergency on our hands. She wasn't moving properly into the birth canal and the contractions were pushing on her strongly due to the absence of fluid. We were beginning to lose her heartbeat, and the umbilical cord had become wrapped around her neck. Our darling baby's heart was failing, she was being choked and we hadn't even had a chance to bring her into the world yet. It was critical to get her stabilized. After a few minutes of frenzied work on behalf of our medical team, her heartbeat was still unstable when I suddenly got the idea that I should be turned on my opposite side. Joy had several monitor wires attached to her in my womb, which made turning me difficult; however, Joy became stabilized and doctors again attempted to deliver her. They tried pulling her out, which didn't work. To her head, they attached a powerful suction cup that, when it broke loose, knocked our doctor off the stool on which she had been sitting. As a last resort, our doctor used forceps for delivery. Although Joy was bruised and battered from her difficult delivery, she arrived in this world healthy as can be and has always lived up to her name.

As one might imagine, she came into this world in a state of panic, screaming her lungs out. At least she was screaming until a nurse handed her to her daddy, who took her gently in his arms and said, "Welcome to the world, Baby Jones. We're glad you're here." Upon hearing his voice, she instantly stopped crying and settled down. Just try to tell me that talking to a baby who is still in the womb has no effect on him or her. I know it does. I've seen the dramatic results myself. Doug and I later learned that at the moment I had suddenly had the idea that I should be turned on my side, our Master Mind group had gathered on our behalf to affirm that the delivery would be one in which guidance and direction would be provided as needed, parents and physicians would know *exactly* what to do in order to provide Joy with a safe delivery into the world, and that all would be well.

Our group was "wowed" to learn what had happened, and so were we.

Never underestimate the power of the mind and never underestimate the power of what the support of your Master Mind group can mean to you. When you are in situations where you can't see the forest for the trees, it is extremely helpful to have those who care about you remain focused on your goal. What you want—wants you. Thoughts are things and they magnetize results to themselves. By aligning yourself with people of like mind, you create a very powerful force.

I felt it shelter to speak to you.

—Emily Dickinson

Without question, the most valuable gift I have received from my Master Mind group is support. When selecting your Master Mind group, choose people who are loving and supportive of you and who do not begrudge you getting what you want out of life.

I have found that the ladder of success is only crowded at the bottom. By choosing to surround myself with positive, successful people who have risen above that level, I don't have to deal with jealousy. There is no competition and there is no back- stabbing. The people in my life understand that there is enough abundance for everyone. Consequently, we all assist each other in achieving our goals rather than stepping on each other to get ahead. There truly is strength in numbers. When you are ready for that kind of wealth in your life, someone will be there to help you get it—if you are aware enough to see them offering you assistance.

It is no mystery to me why the rich get richer and the poor get poorer. It's simply a matter of perspective. You can have the kind of perspective that you want in your life, but it may mean saying good-bye to some old mind-sets because they just don't work anymore.

In looking at getting past the fork in the road, you must first decide what you want to do. Make lists. Revise them until they feel right. Trust your intuition to lead you in the proper direction.

When Doug and I decided to go into business for ourselves, we sat down and listed the qualities we wanted our business to have. We didn't know what kind of business it would be. We just knew the kind of life we wanted. We had both grown tired of working for corporate America and having our destiny in someone else's hands. We had decided, from that day forward, that working for ourselves was the only way we could gain the kind of personal freedom that we wanted to have. So we began to create a mental vision of our business.

We knew we wanted to work together. We wanted more leisure time to enjoy what we knew would one day be a growing family. (At the time, our children had not arrived on the planet.) We wanted a business that would be mobile—meaning that we could do it from anywhere. We wanted it to involve computer technology. We wanted a business that was economically protected and we wanted to travel. Last, but most certainly not least, we wanted to make a substantial income so that we could be free from financial stress and could enjoy the lifestyle of our dreams. In addition, I had a separate goal of wanting a mail-order business, which is a goal I had held in my mind for years. I had always had the vision of money coming to me in the mail from unknown sources. Doug decided that was a vision worth embracing and so we added it to our list.

From this list of qualities, our business began to take form. We knew we were going in the right direction and living our correct purpose because getting our business off the ground went like clockwork.

What have been the results? Together we have built a company that is the nation's premier provider of sales and marketing services to our industry—the mortgage business. Our clients never come to us—we always go to them. Consequently, we are not tied to living in a particular location. We can live anywhere. The business is mobile. As long as I'm within an hour's drive of an airport, we're in business. For the industry, I write several newsletters that have thousands of readers. We live in the country on a lake, hooked up to the world via computer, modem and fax machine. Our business is economically protected. When the economy booms, our business thrives because our services are provided as a bonus to our clients' employees. I speak at annual conventions and we travel to beautiful resort destinations throughout the country. When the economy stinks, our business thrives because clients want me to come in and see if we can get production climbing again. Either way it goes, we win.

Does this sound a lot like the list of qualities we made for our business years ago? It certainly does to me. In fact, the business has manifested itself exactly according to the goals we set.

When we decided that we wanted to start a family, we set the goal that we wanted product sales (books, newsletters, audio and video programs, etc.) to surpass what I made in personal appearances by the time Joy reached kindergarten and wouldn't, therefore, be able to travel with me as much. With strong product sales, I wouldn't have to be on the road so much and could be around more to enjoy her school activities. So we began doing direct-mail marketing.

I recall our first mailing. We did it all ourselves. We couldn't afford to have it printed, so we copied it on our office copier. When our mailing list had finally grown large enough to qualify for bulk mail (200 pieces), we thought we had hit the big time.

Six months before Joy started kindergarten, revenue from product sales surpassed revenue from my personal appearances and it's stayed that way. We now have the largest direct-mail-order business in our industry and our postage bill for one month far exceeds what most people earn in an entire year! It's amazing what can take place in your life when you are clear about what you want to do.

I share this story with you not to be boastful, but to illustrate for you the power of deciding what you want. I'm very sure that *I'm* not the source of this good fortune. There is a force at work here far beyond my power, and what I want you to know is it's available to you as well. When you're living out your right purpose, all the resources of the Universe line up behind you to offer assistance. With that kind of support, you can't lose. However, you do have to put yourself in motion. What you want, wants you—but you have to go get it.

In addition to deciding what you want to do, you must also set forth a plan to accomplish your goals. Don't, under any circumstances, believe that once you set a goal for yourself you can't change it. That just isn't so. Life is always changing and so are you. What's appropriate for you this year may not be next year. You must remain flexible. Goals are very powerful, and having them will enable you to accomplish great things with your life. Goals also have their dangers. Remember: *You control your goals; don't let them control you.* When you adhere stringently to goals that no longer work for you, you are simply trading one rut for another.

Let me give you an example of a goal I'd met that no longer served me.

Shortly after the birth of our son, Andrew, Doug and I decided to move from Denver to Carefree, Arizona. I was sick of snow and I wanted to go to a warmer climate. We had grown tired of living in Denver. The Denver economy was in the depths of economic recession and we had grown weary of being around people who were singing the "blues" all the time. Although our own business was unaffected, we had begun to be affected mentally by the depressed attitude that was prevalent in the community. My husband, a Colorado native, had become disheartened by the level of air pollution in the lovely home of his birth. He had always loved the desert, so a move seemed like a good thing for us to do. So we set a goal of moving to Carefree, Arizona.

Carefree is a beautiful, celebrity-studded community set in the high Sonoran desert, about 30 miles north of the Phoenix/Scottsdale area. It is a golfer's paradise and the scenery, for those who love the desert, is gorgeous. After taking a couple of trips to check out real estate, we finally found our "perfect" property and made our move.

Put this into perspective. Not only did we move, but we also moved our three-year-old daughter, a six-week-old son, a business, office equipment, inventory, and we relocated employees. Not a small move.

At first things seemed fine. However, it didn't take us long to see that we had overlooked one major lifestyle factor—summer! If you've never been through an Arizona summer, you don't know what hot is. We had made one slight mistake. We had only visited Arizona during the winter. Ooops!

People may tell you, "It's a dry heat." Well, so is an oven, but you don't move in. I now know why so many residents of Carefree only lived there four or five months of the year. It is a harsh climate to live in year-round. My children seldom went outside to play. We truly lived in the desert. When they went outside, not only was it frequently hot (the first year we were there, Carefree broke a record for the most number of 100+ degree days that year), but it seemed that everything either stuck them, stung them or bit them. I became well-skilled at scorpion and rattlesnake patrol and I had grossly underestimated how much I would miss grass, trees and water.

Two years after moving there, I knew in my soul that it was not our right place. Aside from the climate, my soul simply was not settled living there. Something was missing, yet I didn't know what it was and I didn't have the heart to say to my husband, "Hey look, I know we've just spent a fortune moving and that we had intended to live here until our children were grown, but I'd really like to move now!" I was afraid he would think I had lost my mind.

When you are not in your right place, signals will come your way. If you're awake to that kind of guidance, you'll pick up on them before too much disaster befalls you. The following were some of our signals: more than 100 days of over 100-degree heat (highest temperature: 123), skyrocketing living expenses, highway construction that made my trips to the airport lengthy and frustrating, three bouts of flash-flooding (our swimming pool overflowed into our living room twice), and near the end of our stay, our house was struck by lightning. Hey, I didn't say the signs were subtle.

Aside from those occurrences, our business had grown by leaps and bounds and we had lost all sense of personal freedom. Our business was running us instead of us running it. We had very little time together as a family. The time we did have was spent with short tempers because we both were totally exhausted. The children were getting short-changed. We weren't having any fun, and on some level we knew it, although no one was saying it. I was burned out. I had been running myself ragged for two years and I was exhausted—physically and mentally. Looking back on it now, I realize that I was on the verge of self-destructing again. Fortunately, we do learn a few things along our path and we "wake up" quicker than we used to in earlier years.

While Doug and I were on a trip, our children had been staying with my parents in Oklahoma. Doug went home to Arizona ahead of me, and I went to Oklahoma to pick them up. When I arrived, I saw them playing joyfully outside, running and scampering, falling down in the grass and generally just loving all that nature had to offer. They were very relaxed and happy. The entire place was laid back and peaceful and suddenly it hit me. I wanted to move home. I wanted to come back to Oklahoma. This was quite a mind stretch for me because I had vowed 20 years ago, when I left the state, that I would NEVER live there again. I realized that beautiful summer afternoon that what was missing in me were my roots. I had left home with a lot of unfinished business. It had taken me 20 years to truly find myself, make myself whole, and develop the strength to live right in the face of things that had controlled my life in the past and to know that they couldn't affect me now.

When I returned home to Arizona from that trip, my husband was sitting out by the pool and, unbeknown to me, had experienced a particularly frustrating day. After gathering my courage, I turned to my husband and said, "If you don't get me out of this place, I'm going to be dead in five years. I want to move home to Oklahoma and I want to slow our life down." This was a major risk for me because I didn't know what his response would be.

My husband turned to me and said, "If I hadn't lived there before, I'd say you were out of your mind. But since I have, and I know how wonderful the people are and what it's like to live there, let's go take a look." We spent the rest of the evening talking about all that had been bothering us, and once again became clear on how we wanted our life to be.

Shortly thereafter we made a trip to Oklahoma to look for real estate. It was our intention to buy some land and to build on it when it "made sense" for us to move. The day we were to start looking for land, my husband *happened* to pick up a magazine in which he saw a home for sale that was on the water. For the heck of it, he asked the Realtor to show it to us.

The instant we walked onto the property, we knew it was ours. Our house sits on a peninsula on a lake, there are more than 100 trees, water can be seen from three sides and the view from the back of the house as the sun sets over the water resembles a scene from the movie *On Golden Pond.*

Down by the lake, there was a hammock strung between two trees at the water's edge. Before going into the house, I lay down in that hammock and I knew my soul had come home to rest. After I had been there about 15 minutes, my husband said, "If we have any hope of getting a reasonable deal on this house, please wipe that smile off your face before the Realtor sees you."

We bought the house on the spot. It took us several months to be able to move into it because we had a lot of business to wrap up in Arizona, but my point in telling you all this is the following: Don't get so locked into your goals that you cut yourself off from something even better that the Universe wants to provide for you. There are times when the achievement of one goal is just a springboard to something more marvelous than you had even imagined. We had no way of knowing our move to Arizona was simply a stopover to prepare us for our "quality of life move" to Oklahoma, where we would be blissfully happy and blessed, but that's what it was.

Since making the move, our family has grown closer, we're happier and business is booming. Only this time, we're running it—not the other way around. We have gained our life back, but it took letting go of one goal so that we could receive something better. A lesson both my husband and I have taken from this experience is that sometimes people cling to the achievement of a goal long after it ceases to serve them simply because they're afraid that if they let go, there won't be anything better to come along. In other words, life blesses you once and that's it. How absurd! We live in an abundant Universe that wants to bless us again and again, so don't be afraid to move on. You were not meant to live in a box labeled "This is my goal. I got it and now there's nothing else."

You own your goals; don't let them own you. Having achieved one goal, life tends to open up others for you. Watch and be open. Your life was meant to be filled with health, wealth, love and joy. If it's lacking in any of those areas, begin to open yourself up to receiving your gift from life to fill the void.

Finally, to bypass the fork in the road and continue on your way, establish a good support system. Surround yourself with people who challenge you to be the best that you can be. Those people won't begrudge you your success. They will help you celebrate it!

FIVE

Using Guilt as Your Guide

Saying Good-bye to Old Habits and Influences

What you are speaks so loudly,
I can't hear what you say.

—Ralph Waldo Emerson

One of the things a man has to learn to fight most bitterly is the influence of those who love him.

—Sherwood Anderson

Just as the oyster endures discomfort and irritation to produce a lovely pearl, so might we be called upon to experience some sadness prior to our joy. What we've been talking about in the previous chapters is setting the stage for personal growth. This kind of growth experience will probably cause a tearing away of old tissue connecting you to the past. However, as with any shackle that binds, the imprisoned will go to great lengths to break the bond to enjoy the gifts of freedom.

We are often heavily vested in the shroud that veils us, which we call our past. Good or bad, it seems to be human nature to want to preserve our past even though it sometimes keeps us from forward movement. Naturally self-destructive? No, I don't think so.

I believe it simply provides us a sense of familiarity—a place in which we feel safe. We know that we made it through our past alive. Even though we had to experience some rough times, we were able to pull through. We now know that we can live up to that level of challenge. There is safety in knowing that and there is comfort in maintaining the status quo. Staying safely connected to the past, for many people, is a preferable alternative to growth. At least there is no perceived risk to them in doing so. Risk to them equates to their security being jeopardized. That evokes a feeling of fear, and fear can be immobilizing. Here we have another description of a rut—fixation on the past.

To break out of your shell and realize your full potential, you must be willing to take a good strong look at your past. You must be willing to sort through the events of your life, learn what you can and discard the rest. You must acknowledge that you are an accumulation of all the events and relationships in your life. Acknowledging those experiences for bringing you into your present form is important. Equally important, however, is choosing to prevent the ghosts from the past from dictating or damaging your future. To be able to do so requires looking at those influences and the portions of your life that they have affected.

Habit and routine have an unbelievable power to waste and destroy.

—Henri De Lubac

If we are going to make a change, we must start with ourselves. Until you say good-bye to the old you, you won't be able to discard the hurtful influence of others from your past. I had allowed much of my life to be ruled by guilt. Therefore, there were three major sets of self-destructive behavior that I needed to say "good-bye" to, so that I could move on with my life. Those influences were:

1. Personal, self-inflicted guilt.
2. "God is gonna' get you" guilt.
3. Guilt from friends and relatives.

Let's begin by looking at our attitudes toward ourselves and how we perceive the world around us.

It has been said that we are a direct result of what we've been told and taught and what we've been sold and bought. How true it is! Each time we buy into a concept, either good or bad, we place another brick into our foundation that we call our belief system. Not everything in that belief system is harmful to us and in need of being discarded. Heavens no! In fact, the majority of it is good and has given you and me the strength and the stamina to be who we are today. However, some of those bricks in our belief system are in definite need of replacement. In fact, when we look back on some of the things we used to believe, they're almost funny. And, who knows, perhaps it's better to laugh about them than to be angry. At least, it seems to feel better. Let me cite a personal example.

I used to have a recurring cycle in my life that played itself out repeatedly until I finally noticed that I was the only constant in the situation and, therefore, I must be the cause.

The cycle to which I'm referring had to do with two "bricks" in my belief system. One had to do with the concept of what it meant to be a successful woman. The other had to do with a money rejection complex, and yet the two were interwoven into the same repetitive cycle of behavior.

Here's what would occur. I would struggle and struggle to succeed, and then when I made it, I did everything within my power to undermine my accomplishments so that I would have to start all over again. When this began to happen to me for the third time, for whatever reason, it dawned on me that the repetitive cycle had something to do with my belief system and that if I wanted to break the cycle, I'd better figure out where the problem was and fix it.

Oklahoma and Texas, two states in which I've lived many years of my life, are heavily steeped in Southern attitudes. While growing up, I had learned that there were only certain "acceptable" occupations for women to pursue. Teaching, nursing and secretarial work were a few. I recall someone encouraging me to take typing classes, so that in the event ("God forbid") anything should happen to my husband, and I was left to care for the children on my own, I would have a skill to fall back upon. I can't, for the life of me, remember who told me that, but it stuck.

I doubt that it was intended for me to take the message away from those attitudes that I did, but here's how I interpreted those social customs. I told myself that it was okay for a woman to go into business, but not to be too successful at it. In other words, a woman could go into business as a means of survival, but not as a means of fulfillment. So, when my business became "too" successful, I would knock it back down into the struggle stage. I had bought the concept that a woman's role in business was about survival, not about winning, because everyone knows that if a woman goes into business and becomes too successful, she will turn into a brazen hussy, she'll be unattractive and she'll have a hard time catching a man!

In rural settings such as the one in which I grew up, catching a man is not just a passing thought, it's a major life's occupation. Where I'm from, if you find somebody you're not related to, you marry him! This sounds exaggerated and silly, I know, but many of the belief systems that hold us back aren't rooted in reality but in distortion. Sometimes when we look back on what we used to believe, it makes us laugh. But it's no laughing matter at the time you're struggling with it, is it?

The second "brick" causing me trouble was a money rejection complex. As a result of my religious upbringing, I had put it into my head that somehow money was bad. I had been raised on quotations such as "It's easier for a camel to pass through the eye of a needle than for a rich man to enter into heaven" and "Money is the root of all evil," etc. I had learned that to want a lot of money was not good. Consequently, when my efforts produced more money than my "deserve" level would allow me to enjoy, I'd knock myself back down to the place where I felt comfortable. It took me years to overcome the money rejection complex and become comfortable with money.

We all have portions of our belief systems that can cause us trouble if we don't re-evaluate them periodically throughout our adulthood. In order for you to grow in your life, you need to look at what's been holding you back and lessen its influence on your life.

Another big triumph for me was coming to terms with who I thought I was supposed to be and then putting it into perspective. By putting the idea of who I thought I was supposed to be to rest, and instead finding out who I *wanted* to be, I realized that most of those "supposed to" beliefs were nothing more than habits that weren't serving me very well. Knowing that gave me the courage to move ahead by realizing that if I had the power to cultivate those habits, I certainly had the power to change them. It's amazing to me that when we get sick and tired of repeating the same cycles over and over, we can often change our habits quickly. I believe that when our motivation is strong enough, we can accomplish virtually anything.

Bad habits are easier to abandon today than tomorrow.

—Yiddish proverb

As a child I had been trained to accept standards that constituted the way a "good" person behaved.

However, as a teenager I began to think for myself and no longer accepted those standards as appropriate for me. I had always found them unrealistic and stifling.

Tradition played a major role in my life, as it does in many people's lives. We may mold ourselves to who our parents and family tell us we are "supposed" to be, or we may go to the other extreme. The other end of the spectrum holds many of us who have found it necessary to completely rebel against all that we have been taught. Both of these extremes are hurtful because they suppress the real you. Somewhere in the middle, between total conformity and massive rebellion, lies your natural state. Finding that balance makes the difference between a peaceful, joyful life and total neurosis.

Whichever end of the spectrum you have placed yourself on doesn't really matter. What matters is knowing that you chose to be where you are today.

That statement won't sit well with a lot of people, and that's okay. It's much easier for us to say that others have made us be the way we are or that circumstances have shaped us. That simply is not the truth. In order to grow beyond where you are now, you must be willing to take responsibility for yourself. You must acknowledge that the game of blame-placing is over. This may not be easy. It's safer to be the victim or the martyr of circumstance. After all, how could anyone blame you or hold you responsible for things when you are so powerless? Right? Wrong!

Get out of the habit of giving away the power in your life to others. You're not Pinocchio. The only strings attached to you are there by your own design. If you've got a puppeteer controlling your life, it's because you felt the need to hire one. It's much easier to stop those habits now than it will be 10 years from now. You see, the longer habits survive, the stronger they become and the more power you lose.

Only the suppressed word is dangerous.

—Ludwig Borne

My strict Southern Baptist upbringing created resentment in my life. It's not my intention to send up red flares of anger to people who adhere to that religious philosophy. Those theologies and beliefs work for many people, and I respect that. They weren't suitable for me. The rejection of that way of life started a series of self-defeating habits for me that took years and years to change, with many lessons learned along the way. To reject that religious background meant, in many respects, that I was turning my back on family tradition, and that wasn't easy for me to do. Ways of life for most of my family members were dictated by generations of behavior. Things were the way they were just because that's the way they had always been. Although I am an only child, my extended family is very large—as is true of most families in farming communities. They are, for the most part, wonderful, loving people. Looking back on our lives now, however, it is easy to see the unnecessary pain we have inflicted upon ourselves and each other by adhering to tradition and self-righteous morality, setting unachievable standards and living in hypocrisy.

I have learned to take responsibility for my personal attitude. This lesson was very difficult for me because I had to release a lot of anger and resentment.

It sometimes surprises me to see how unwilling we are to let go of anger because it seems we have somehow developed a strange affection for it. It provides us with comfort and rationale for our unloving behavior. Anger frequently prevents us from sharing our love with those who are so dear to us.

It is vital to our growth for us to realize that no one *makes* us be, do, act or behave in a certain manner. *We* choose how we respond to situations. That is now and always has been the case. This is a difficult concept for most people to understand. We prefer to believe that we are creatures of our environment. We tend to accept that we are generally *reacting* to others rather than *acting* independently on our own. How often have you heard yourself or others around you say "I just can't help it" or "I can't do anything about it" or "That's just the way things are," etc.? This is a self-defeating habit. The more you buy into it, the less you will enjoy your life because you will always believe that things are beyond your control.

At times it is difficult for us to see what we're doing to ourselves. Self-defeating habits flourish in an environment that is lacking in awareness. They take you over slowly—often going unnoticed. You might succumb to the self-defeating habits, or your inner self will rise up one day, destroy the power of these habits, and make drastic changes in your life.

In the midst of my formative years, I did not notice the habit patterns being established in my mind that would later cause me pain as an adult. In the beginning of this chapter I said, "If we are going to make a change, we must start with ourselves. . . ." So, start with myself I did.

My childhood contained a tremendous amount of turmoil and my family unit broke up repeatedly. When I was nine years old, my parents divorced. They probably should have taken that measure many years before because neither was happy. My parents had begun being boyfriend and girlfriend when they were in grade school. They married shortly after graduating from high school and neither of them had had the opportunity to define who they were, separate from each other. Consequently, as they grew into their adult roles, they grew apart rather than together. They simply got married too young and had not yet experienced enough of life.

Although they should have divorced much sooner, the tradition and morality of the time was of the "Until death do we part" vintage. As a result, they created hell on earth for one another. Their divorce was devastating to me.

After my father left home, the discipline and strictness my mother imposed upon me seemed to escalate. My mother felt that she had been a doormat for my dad and she was bound and determined that I wasn't going to be that way. Their divorce also presented a number of morality issues and it was a given that, in our household, we would walk the "straight and narrow." I began to feel a great deal of tension. Adding to that tension was my growing sense of feeling responsible for whether or not my mother experienced happiness. I began to set a trap in which I caught myself. On the one hand I wanted to rebel, on the other hand I wanted to please. It's difficult to have a foot on each side of the fence, and it is a tremendous burden when you try to take on the responsibility of being the source of someone else's happiness.

For many years, I suffered from what I call the Perfect Child Syndrome. I have found that many people have created something similar in their lives. According to Elisabeth Kubler-Ross, world renowned for her work with the terminally ill, we in Western society have raised many generations of children who believe in the "I'll love you if" theory. The theory goes something like this, "I'll love you if you: are quiet, good-looking, athletic, well mannered; make good grades; do what I say, etc." She contends that we raise our children believing they must be superhuman in order to merit our approval, and thus our love.

That was a message I had bought into wholeheartedly. The Perfect Child Syndrome was something I created for myself to cope with unpleasant situations. It was effective in handling those ordeals. The problem was that in later years, it had gotten out of hand. I couldn't figure out how to get myself out of this self-created syndrome.

Stress, anger, bitterness and tension are conflicts that I have never dealt with well. The best way for me to cope with those feelings was to avoid them. Consequently, at a very early age I designated myself to be the family court jester. I felt it was my responsibility to keep everyone smiling and happy. Little did I know the kind of pressure I was creating for myself and the heavy burden of responsibility I had undertaken. You see, we like to have our load lightened.

If you offer to do that for people, they'll let you. Then the next thing you know, they begin to expect it from you.

Martyrs express anger lovingly.

—Lee Gibson

This whole process began at an early age, when I somehow decided that because of me my parents weren't getting along. Despite their assurances to the contrary, that is what I believed. I quickly discovered I could put a halt to an argument by being funny or acting out crazy characters. I learned how to be a masterful salesman! It was easy for me to persuade others to trade conflict for a smile, even if it only lasted for a little while. In my adolescent years, when most of what I did and wanted was met with disapproval, I learned to gain approval by making good grades, winning awards and basically being Little Miss Goody Two Shoes. The tragedy of the situation was that at some point (I'm not sure just when), I actually started to believe that *all* of that outstanding performance was necessary. I actually believed that if I didn't make all those super achievements, I had somehow lost some value and those dear to me would be disappointed. How distorted.

Consequently, I began beating up on myself if I didn't live up to my expectations. I felt guilty if I didn't make excellent grades, win first place in everything

I did and always behave sweetly. That carried over into my adult life also. I made sure that I molded myself into what I thought was an acceptable form to those I loved—even if it meant denying what I really wanted, even if it meant making myself unhappy. I made sure that to the outside world, everything appeared just wonderful. I was the classic example of a china doll that looks great on the outside, but is empty on the inside.

The pressure you put yourself under when you behave that way is intense. I felt responsible for the happiness of everyone who was dear to me. What was really happening, however, was that I was living my life for everyone but *me*. The first time anyone "called" me on this game was during my senior year in high school. Of course, I was shocked. I felt sure I had my image under control. That year I was co-editor of the yearbook, captain of the cheerleading squad, a member of the Honor Society, Girls State Rep, winner of the Award of Excellence in Piano Guild, vice president of the senior class and held various club officer positions. However, much to my surprise, a teacher who knew me well wrote in my yearbook, "To Debra—the clown always there to make everyone smile, but crying all the time on the inside." For the *first* time I realized someone else knew that I didn't know how to escape the trap I'd set for myself—and how really miserable I was.

That was a turning point for me. I decided to set myself free from all the guilt and pressure I had put on myself. The unraveling of the web did not occur overnight. It took me five years to reach the place where I completely released myself from the obligation of being responsible for others. One reason it was not easy was because when you allow yourself to be linked with the happiness of others, you also leave yourself open to their guilt. They will exert the influence of guilt on you to get you to continue to behave in a manner that is pleasing to them. The bottom line is that just because you're ready to quit doesn't mean they're ready for you to stop. I had to come to the realization that if my failure to be "perfect" upset them, that was their problem. I believed it was time they grew up and became self-sufficient also. I believed that it was time they created their own happiness rather than being dependent on me.

Once we realize that people must be in charge of their own lives and no one else can do it for them, it enables us to re-channel that energy into something more positive. Personal, self-inflicted guilt trips have become good guideposts for me. Now, when I am aware that I'm beating up on myself, my new level of awareness automatically kicks in. It provides me with an opportunity to look at the situation objectively, weigh the consequences of my self-abuse and then move on. Generally I find that the things I'm giving myself a hard time about are insignificant. It's just my old habit patterns coming through to try and convince me that I can't accomplish my goal. To make the influence of those patterns diminish or go away, I take my mind off the problems and put it onto the solutions. That always makes me feel less unworthy and more powerful.

I realize that much of what my mother and I went through were independence wars. I remember my mother telling me over and over again, "You're not going to be like I was. You're going to be smart, and you're going to be independent and you're going to be able to take care of yourself." I also remember in my early teen years my mother said, "I think we've taken this independence thing a bit too far." At that point it was a little late. My strong will was very well developed.

After my parents' divorce, it seemed to me as though my mother felt she had some debt to pay or that there was something out of balance that needed to be set right, and she was going to force me to be "good." My mother made sure we were in church all the time, doing the right things to make us "good" people. "Shoulds," "oughts" and "have tos" were a large part of the vocabulary I heard. Manipulation through guilt was a powerful tool. I resented having a philosophy forced on me that I didn't agree with, and at the same time I felt guilty for feeling that way.

The message I interpreted from the pulpit was that the majority of the things I was interested in, enjoyed and dreamed about were going to send me directly to hell. There, I would burn for eternity in payment for my sins.

The devil made me do it.

—Flip Wilson

It astounds me to see how many lives are riddled with guilt from the religious philosophies adults were forced to believe as children. Many people become immobilized because they feel whatever they do may put them out of favor with God. This is particularly true for those who follow fundamentalist religions. In my opinion, these religions border on superstition because it's only when people are kept in submission and fear of "the wrath of God" that the religion maintains its influence.

The self-righteous judgment of one's peers prevents many people from deciding, on their own, whether or not their religion is right for them. Instead, they just accept that that's the way things are, and if they can't live up to the expectations or if they question the religious doctrines, they deserve to be "cast out." In some philosophies, having a mind of your own and questioning doctrine is blasphemy.

I've questioned things all my life and it's not popular with a lot of people. It's much easier to control someone who accepts things the way they are instead of questioning them.

Spirituality has always been a central issue for civilized man. Whether or not you have one religious belief or another is irrelevant. The question is, are you comfortable with your beliefs as an *adult?*

You owe it to yourself to determine what the order of the Universe means to you, without relying on the decisions you've made as a child. Chances are, those decisions were influenced by authority figures. But by being well-informed and by studying the philosophies and religions of the world, you can determine what is best for you. I've known since I was small that my life would be about impacting hundreds of thousands of people, that I would be financially well off and that I would achieve a degree of fame. When people know that about themselves, they tend to be a little different. I have found that children with that kind of drive tend to dream a lot, they tend to live in the future more than they live in the present, they tend to relate more to people who are older than they are, and they're perfectionistic. You wrap all of that together and you're bound to have a person who feels a little different from everyone else.

Musical ability was always a long suit for me. I was always the first person asked to sing or play for various functions throughout my community. With this talent came an intense desire to be in show business. So I entered into forbidden territory. Baptists don't believe in drinking or dancing. I was in trouble! My dream was to be a famous singer with a band. There are not many bands who perform in places where drinking and dancing are prohibited, unless they are religious groups. Being a gospel singer didn't inspire me at all. Consequently, I repressed my dream and my resentment grew.

My life seemed to be terribly out of balance. It was filled with can'ts and nos. As I recall my teen years, I can still hear certain phrases ringing loud and clear. "No, you can't go to the dance." "No, you can't go to that party—their parents drink." "No, you can't stay out past 10 o'clock." "No, you can't have a bikini, they're vulgar." "Don't sass me." "Because I said so, that's why." "You're grounded." On and on it went. I felt like I was choking. These Puritanical views were just widening the gap between myself and my peers. I felt peculiar and embarrassed, so I compensated by being a super achiever.

Although I felt a lot of rebellion inside, I found myself complying with all the rules in order to ease the consequence, and hating it all along. The compliance nevertheless continued and the resentment grew. Consequently, the night I graduated from high school I moved. After I graduated from college, I left my home state, vowing never to return, and for the next 20 years lived in various cities throughout the country. As unfortunate as it may seem, sometimes distance is required in order for us to break the chains of influence and find out who we really are.

People who fly into a rage always make a bad landing.

—Will Rogers

The night I graduated from high school and moved, I gained something I had been desperately seeking—freedom. Something for which I had yearned for years was finally mine. At last the opportunity was mine to express who I *really* was, rather than trying to fit someone else's idea of who I *should* be. For so many years I had been conducting a silent rebellion within myself, and resentment had built up a tremendous force. Therefore, when I experienced this newfound freedom, I attacked life at an incredible speed. My appetite was voracious for living and experiencing what the world had to offer. The pendulum had swung to the other extreme and life was once again out of balance. The habit pattern of living life in an out-of-balance fashion was still there, just as it had been when I was living under my mother's rule. The only thing that had changed was direction.

Ten years came and went while I lived life out of balance, until it occurred to me I still wasn't living life on *my* terms. It still wasn't working. In looking at the reasons why, it became evident to me that I had developed a strong habit of rationalizing my current behavior based on the resentment I felt from deprivation in my earlier years.

When I felt I didn't measure up, I blamed it on lack of exposure. Anytime I overindulged, my rationalization for it was that I overcompensated to fill that need, based on having been deprived of those activities in earlier years. I promised myself I would do better next time and not go to extremes. The habit of blaming behavior on someone or something other than myself was well established. I was taking true responsibility for very little in my life. Consequently, my life was not under my control. It was going off like a loose cannon and it wasn't moving in the directions I wanted. Things seemed to be falling apart. I wondered why.

It's important to note that all of this was an internal struggle. External appearances indicated a successful, well-established businesswoman, happily married, well-adjusted and full of zest for living. What a facade! The earth-shaking revelation was about to come to me that my life's problems couldn't be blamed on my mother, my father or anyone else for that matter—just me.

For the first time in my life I realized that it was time to deal with the issues of my past and then say good-bye to the old me. It was time for me to live my life as an independent adult, free from guilt and resentment. I was finally *ready* to learn who I was. The reason I say "ready" is that it takes being sick of the way things are to make a change, and it takes courage to accept the fact that you are the *only one* in control of your life. There is no one else you can blame. Any unpleasant experiences you may have encountered in your life are irrelevant. What's important is how you chose to let them affect you. Shirley MacLaine expressed it well when she said, "You must go out on a limb to get the fruit."

Some of you may be thinking it's absurd to go back through your formative years and bring all the ghosts out of the closet. To those of you who hold that opinion, all I can say to you is you will never be free and in control of your life until you do! I work with hundreds of people each year who are adults who have *never* grown up. A single phone call from a family member with a little bit of guilt-ridden innuendo can send these supposedly grown adults running around like little scattered chickens in an effort to "please." For some people, manipulation through guilt is strong. Take hold of the reins of your life and do what you want because you want to, not because you want to placate someone. You will create a cycle of doing deeds to please people that only creates within you resentment, hate and self-repression—all of which are debilitating habit patterns.

More important, they will keep you from truly loving those people you're trying so desperately to please. Guilt and love cannot reside within the same framework. Guilt and obligation maybe, but not guilt and love. Don't short-change yourself. By openly loving the dear ones in your life without guilt, you will be experiencing one of the most enriching aspects of your life. It may be one of the only times you've loved them for who they are, not because of the demands they place on you. I have a love for my mother now that I would have been incapable of having before. She is an extraordinary woman whom I love and respect. It took me a long time to realize that she was just doing the best she could with me, and to let that go. Now it was my turn to do the best I could. *You* must set yourself free; no one can do it for you.

The last of personal freedoms of which no one can deprive you is choice.

—Dr. Victor Frankel

We have a choice regarding our personal attitudes. It's up to us how we greet each and every day and it's important that we share our lives with people who build us up rather than tear us down. I call those people who tear you down friends you can't afford. Have you noticed that to function in today's fast-paced society requires a lot of energy? Have you noticed that there are people in the world that don't feel quite alive unless they've created about a half-dozen traumas before 10 A.M.? These people aren't looking for answers. They are the chronic whiners, moaners and complainers and they'll drain the life right out of you if you're not careful.

If you'd like to limit the influence of those kind of people in your life, you may have an interest in a philosophy I adopted a number of years ago.

I made a decision to eradicate negativity from my life. Over the years, I've received a lot of criticism from people for taking this point of view. People have said things to me like, "Oh, Debra, you're such a Pollyanna; you think just because you think happy thoughts, happy things are going to happen. Get real! You don't work with the people I work with." "You believe that because you expect everyone to cooperate and be fair that that's what's going to take place. Get a grip!" "You think that just because you've decided that we're all going to get on the Success Train that we're just going to line up and take our places and we'll go chugging happily along the track."

Do I really think that? No, of course I don't. Does your decision to eradicate negativity from your life mean that the gripers, whiners, moaners and complainers in your life suddenly go "POOF" and vanish from the planet? No, absolutely not. In fact, you can count on them to show up every day. It's hard to get rid of these people because they're on a mission to spread misery and they don't want to leave you out.

So, if negative people are still in your life, how can you possibly eradicate negativity from your existence? What does eradicating negativity mean? It means that you no longer participate in its perpetuation.

With that thought in mind, the next time you see the chronic complainers coming your way, I want you to see a green neon sign flashing on their forehead that reads, *Energy Sucker, Energy Sucker.* As they begin to sing the "Ain't It Awful Song" of which they know 112,000 verses, politely excuse yourself and walk away. Remember: These people aren't looking for answers. What are they looking for? An audience. When the audience begins to disappear, they will get the point that they haven't been a delight to be around and they'll either self-correct, or they'll figure you're no fun anymore and they'll complain to someone else. In either instance, your day-to-day environment will improve dramatically because you won't have to witness the spewing of their poison anymore.

So the next time someone makes you angry or tries to lay a guilt trip on you, remember you have choices. You can let that person disrupt your entire day and upset you, or you can choose to excuse yourself and not deal with him or her. When people lose the ability to suck you into their trauma, you become a very powerful individual. You are controlling your life rather than being controlled and victimized by others.

Some things, of course, you can't change. Pretending that you have is like painting stripes on a horse and hollering 'Zebra!'

—Eddie Cantor

Gaining control of your own attitude will bring about changes in your relationships. There are people in your life that you don't always feel comfortable with. You will begin to know why. When listening to a friend or relative gripe and complain, you will realize that you don't feel better having spent time with that person. Knowing that you are in control of your life, you will begin to decide to spend less time with those people. Whether overtly, or covertly, it will begin to happen. The same will be true of relationships you have with people who, in the past, have laden you with guilt. Being a self-directed person, you will begin choosing to limit your association with those individuals who are liabilities rather than assets to you and the positive life you are building. This is what I mean by, "To say good-bye begins the journey." Slowly you will find your circle of friends is changing. You will serve as a magnet, pulling people toward you that are like you and your new way of life. You will also repel those who are not like you. Consequently, their influence upon you will lessen.

It isn't so much that hard times are coming; the change observed is mostly soft times going.

—Groucho Marx

Taking this step is generally not easy in the beginning. We are afraid of hurting people's feelings if we really level with them. We're afraid that if we're truly honest about how we feel toward their behavior, the damage will be irreparable and we will lose their love and caring. You must keep in mind that the only person you can be responsible for is you. All you can do is be truthful in how you feel. It is up to them how they choose to respond. You have *nothing* to do with that. Don't try to be so superior as to predetermine outcome for them. No one is capable of doing that for another. Give *them* the opportunity to grow as well.

Saying good-bye to old friends, relatives and influence is not easy, but it's worth it if you really want to get out of your rut. Bob Trask, who has a wonderful set of tapes called *Winning All the Time*, talks about growing beyond your friends and loved ones. He tells a story that I believe graphically illustrates the crossroads you will meet, and the question that must be answered.

The story is about the Mexican fishermen who fish in the Gulf Stream waters for crabs. Every day they take their wire baskets and wade into the water to gather their catch, which they will sell. One day a fisherman was at a dock cleaning his equipment and a tourist walking by said, "I see you wade out into the water with wire baskets to catch crabs, but there's something I don't understand. These wire baskets are not that big and they're open at the top. What keeps the crabs from just crawling out over the top of the basket and going back into the sea where they belong?" The fisherman looked up at him, smiled and said, "Well, the key is you never put just one crab into the basket, because the crab will crawl out over the basket and go back into the sea where he belongs. You always put in at least two crabs. Then, as one crab begins to crawl out, his friends will pull him back down."

The question is, do you have any crabs in your life? If you've got people in your life who are not treating you the way you want to be treated or supporting you in the way you want to be supported, you can change it. You know that old cliché, "Kill 'em with kindness"? That holds a great deal of truth. If you want people to treat you differently, start treating them the way you want to be treated. The "kill 'em with kindness" routine will either drive them bananas and they will leave your life, or they'll change. Either way, your situation is improved. Sometimes it's difficult for us to let go of old relationships. Just keep in mind that it wasn't working. If your growth causes someone to feel the need to leave your life, just remember that it's best for both of you and then move forward.

In talking with people in various careers, there is a common story that I hear. Many people who are experiencing success have one or more persons in their life that seem to create obstacles and be a detriment to that person's success. When that happens to us, it has a tendency to make us angry. We find ourselves saying things like, "You just don't understand the pressure I'm under." "Yes, I do have to work on Saturday." "If you just knew what I'm going through," etc. We begin to feel misunderstood and unappreciated when it appears that those around us are making things harder on us. There is a truth that I believe gener- ally applies to these people. When people seem to be trying to hold you down by not understanding you or by trying to make you feel guilty with statements such as "Who do you think you are, some kind of big shot?" or "What's the matter, did your phone break? I never hear from you anymore. Guess you've become too good for your old friends," don't get angry. Try looking at the situation from another angle.

It has been my experience that these people are operating from fear. The bottom line of what they're saying to you is that they're afraid you're going to grow and change so much that you'll run off and leave them behind. You generally go through some changes as success enters your life, and those around you may feel threatened. They may feel like they can't keep up with your growth, and so they begin to try to hold you down at the level where they feel comfortable. The only way they know how to do that is by sometimes creating roadblocks for you.

When viewed from this perspective, it's easier to understand. Rather than attacking back, which would only increase the chasm between you, treat them with love and try to encompass them in what you're doing. If you choose to respond with love instead of anger, it's easier to detach yourself from their emotional entanglements—the webs in which they try to capture you. It's easier to know that you're growing as fast as you can and you'd like to take them with you, but only they can decide to grow with you. Not everyone wants to grow. That's a harsh reality to accept, but it's true and sometimes we have to just let that be.

The enthusiastic, to those who are not, are always something of a trial.

—Alban Goodier

By putting into practice the philosophies and principles found in this book, your life will take on new meaning, excitement and direction. You will find yourself accomplishing your dreams at an incredibly rapid pace. Success in your endeavors will come to you easier and more quickly each and every time you attempt a new challenge. Be prepared to accept that not everyone is going to be happy for you.

Apathetic America is alive and well. People are accustomed to moving with the masses or blending with the crowd. The few rare individuals, like yourself, who are willing to break away from the crowd and try things a different way are almost an affront to the general public. Mediocrity is so well entrenched in our society that expansion and new, outrageous ideas are often viewed as a threat to personal security, safety and comfort. When people feel attacked, they will usually retaliate.

As you experience your new growth and identity, you will probably want to share it with your friends and loved ones. If they are open, self-secure individuals, they may support you in your new endeavors and offer you their excitement and assistance. If they feel threatened by the "new you," you may suddenly find yourself surrounded by critics. The reason for this is that you are excelling in an area where they feel inadequate. Otherwise, they would not respond so strongly. That being the case, they generally do not have the openness and personal reserves upon which to draw to allow you to be who you are. Consequently, their only recourse is to attack and belittle your pursuits. This returns to them some sense of the power they feel they lost when you progressed ahead of them. It's classic "one-up-manship."

Often we attack and make ourselves enemies, to conceal that we are vulnerable.

—Friedrich Nietzsche

Few people in this world will tell you the truth about why they criticize you. Criticism can be viewed as the tip of the iceberg. The critical response is just the outward manifestation of the anger, hurt, resentment or paranoia that they feel deep inside. Just like children who taunt a child on the playground by calling that child "four eyes" or "fatso" to cover up for the fact they're not as intelligent as that child, adults do the same thing to one another. The only thing that really changes is our style and our vocabulary. The intent is the same. Someone is made to feel bad because that person excelled. As adults we've learned to camouflage that intent, to be more subtle—and thus more destructive.

Some people elevate themselves by putting others down and standing on them.

—Lee Gibson

When you encounter people who are not exactly thrilled with your new way of living, you will find that they respond to you in various ways. Some people can only make themselves feel better by putting you down and criticizing you. Their hope is that you will begin to question yourself and stop your new endeavor. If they can successfully stop your progress, then you have no choice but to return to where you were. Back to where *they* felt comfortable.

I am familiar with this type of behavior. A graphic example of it was displayed by a man I was dating years ago. By nature, I am a cheerful person. Being happy is my natural state. I always try to see the optimistic side of things, and most people who meet me say I am an effervescent person. This man was Mr. Negativity and he had just about zero appreciation for my constant cheerfulness. So his attempt to bring me down was to question me regularly about my attitude. At times I felt the only way it could have been more like an interrogation was if I had had a floodlight in my face. He would say, "I can't believe you're *always* this way." "What are you covering up?" "This doesn't seem natural. Why are you being so fake with me?" "Nobody can be this happy all the time." He continued on and on until I started to question whether I was really happy or just acting. I searched my soul for some major character flaw. Fortunately, my new awareness kicked in and I thought, "Wait a minute, Bucko! If you're miserable, that's too bad. You're not going to drag me down in the quagmire with you!" The decision was easy to make. We sat down and had a heart-to-heart discussion. I got right to the crux of the matter and told him the reason I felt he badgered me about being happy was that he was so unhappy he couldn't bear to see anyone without his problem. The contrast was too painful. Like I told you before, people can't argue with the truth. They are so unaccustomed to hearing it that its effect is stunning.

Much to my surprise, he agreed that was the problem and we never had those discussions again. I could have just as easily allowed him to get to me and change my attitude. Be aware when personal attacks and criticism come your way. Remember, how you respond is up to you. If somebody doesn't like a part of you, it's probably because you're acting like a mirror, reflecting a fault about the person that he or she doesn't wish to acknowledge.

Envy is thin because it bites but never eats.

—Spanish proverb

Another method people sometimes use is to try to break your spirit with guilt. This ties in very closely with the discussion earlier in the book regarding friends and loved ones holding you down because they're afraid you're going to run off and leave them. Fear like that is one source of guilt manipulation. The other is envy and/or jealousy. These are very powerful emotions and can overtake them. They may feel that the only option they have to keep you from getting ahead is to immobilize you with guilt. For people who are very close to us, this is an incredibly effective tool.

These people are in a desperate situation. They want what you're getting, but they don't know how to get it. So rather than ask you, they try to destroy your efforts by making you feel sorry for them.

I once had a friend who was very dear to me but who was quite jealous of my expanding life. When we met we had many experiences in common and therefore many stories to share. There was a time when we spent a considerable number of hours together. That began changing. There were some basic differences between us that made those changes inevitable. Differences such as: positive attitude vs. negative attitude, aggressiveness vs. complacency, search for self-knowledge and growth vs. acceptance of lot in life, and multiplicity of friendship circles vs. singularity of contact.

As my business and personal life evolved and expanded, we grew further apart. This person became increasingly dependent on me for emotional stability and support. It was not uncommon for me to receive a call asking that I cancel my plans and come rushing to this person's side to prevent the person from "breaking." This cycle continued to perpetuate itself to the point of discussion of suicide. (No life-threatening attempts were ever made.) I finally realized all of this was a ploy to prevent me from moving forward. The effect all of this had on my performance was detrimental. I had become very reactive to statements such as, "Well, if you just had a little bit of time you could spare me. . . ." Statements like that are just dripping with guilt. When I became aware of the game that was being played, it was easy to stop. The next "suicide" call I got I responded by saying, "I'd be happy to help you if you want to help yourself.

However, this suicide thing is getting the best of both of us. I believe you do this just to get my attention and that is not necessary. You would see me more if you weren't so dismal to be around. I've decided that if this has to kill one of us, it isn't going to be me!"

An amazing thing happened—it didn't kill that person, either. We had some straightforward talks about jealousy and envy after that and we now have a much stronger relationship than before. When it comes right down to it, people are generally very strong. It's only when we insist on helping them that they remain helpless. I've learned an extremely valuable lesson as a result of friends and relatives who have tried to make me feel guilty through the years. Sometimes people you value can tell you your ideas are crazy and absurd long enough that you actually start to believe them. I have learned that when everyone's telling me I'm crazy, I'm on the right track. People are often afraid to break out of their mold. It's safe to them, so of course they're going to think you're crazy for breaking out on your own path. They probably couldn't even entertain the thought. Just know how special you are and keep moving forward. You don't have to agree with someone to love them. Remember that.

Handling guilt from friends and relatives can work for you. You can gain personal power and increased freedom by refusing to allow their criticism to offend you. When the energy is drained from the critical situation, the person who is criticizing you no longer gets the payoff. They don't get the powerful feeling they expected. They are forced to realize they can't dictate your actions by their influence, so they will eventually stop trying. That gives you freedom. You can also keep yourself from moving backwards by not succumbing to guilt. Take that guilt-filled situation and use it as a guidepost. Just know that if they felt it was important enough to lay a guilt trip on you, you must be very close to succeeding and accomplishing your objective. Otherwise, they wouldn't bother.

If we cannot be happy and powerful and prey on others, we invent conscience and prey on ourselves.

—Elbert Hubbard

When you break the spell of the past, you will feel phenomenal energy and a renewed spirit for living. It's as though you are discovering yourself and your own personal power for the first time. Don't let pangs of conscience destroy your momentum. There will be those who will prey on you with strong emotional shockwaves. They will try to make you feel badly for the changes you are making. Do not listen. This is an illusion they fabricate to try to keep you from leaving them. They don't have the courage to expand and grow, so they don't want you to, either. Do not accept that guilt. Let them go with love. Invite them to come along with you, but don't turn back if they don't.

If, at this point, you allow someone to keep you from doing something that you know is right for you, you are creating a rut in which you allow others to control your life. This rut allows you to remain safe because to grow would mean losing so-and-so; at least that's how you rationalize it to yourself. In reality, if so-and-so doesn't care enough about you to let you be who you are, you don't have much of a relationship anyway. I realize there are those who would rather sell their soul than be alone, but believe me, there are much worse things than being alone—giving up on your life is one. The irony is that those who choose to give up and live according to someone else's definitions, usually end up feeling alone, even though they have that other person in their life because a part of their soul is gone. Do you want that to happen to you? No, I didn't think so.

SIX

You Are Everything You Need

How to Create the Life of Your Dreams

If children could be taught only one thing, they should be taught that this is a mental world.

—Emmet Fox

Most folks are about as happy as they make up their minds to be.

—Abraham Lincoln

This chapter contains the secret to having everything you want. Other chapters in this book share with you my personal philosophies of life as they have developed as a result of my own experience. This chapter differs in that not only are the philosophies presented here my own, but they are also those of great minds through the ages. Truths remain unchanged and continue to weave themselves through the fabric of generation after generation. It has been said that Truth persists. I believe that is so.

What I am about to share with you on the next few pages has been the largest catalyst for change in my life. It has allowed me to tap a power I heretofore would have called miraculous. I now call it the natural law of the Universe. Throughout the course of time, the practice of these concepts has helped giants emerge from the most humble beginnings. This subject could be discussed with so much fervor and enthusiasm that one might view it as fanatical. I shall restrain from such extremes of expression because I know that society as a whole discounts the words of zealots. This is far too important to be jeopardized, so you will have this explained to you in a very logical, rational and methodical approach. The great truths are very simple and yet we don't understand how to apply them to our lives. You see, we are so often entrenched in the belief that "Life is tough." Trust me. It is not. The time has come to break out of the "life is tough" rut. It no longer serves you.

Few really believe. The most only believe that they believe.

—John Lancaster Spalding

Most people go through life accepting that for "some reason" they can't have the things they want. The reason they don't have what they want in their lives is that *they don't believe they can have it.* That's all.

The chapters leading up to this one have been preparing you to understand the next few pages. The majority of us have been raised with Western cultural values that tell us life is lived within limits. The truth is, life is limitless. All the abundance and wealth of the Universe that you can handle is there right now waiting for you. To unlock the door to that storehouse, however, you must take off the filters that have blurred your vision. You must find out what you truly believe—not what someone else told you to believe. When you achieve that you will have reached your starting place. If you will put into practice the ideas contained in this chapter, it could more appropriately be called your launching pad.

Taking off the filters means:

1. Realizing what your life has been.
2. Determining what your dreams are.
3. Getting rid of obstacles and people who have been holding you down.

If you're not finished dealing with garbage from your past, don't use it as an excuse for not starting this new way of living. Rare are the individuals who can complete that process before they begin this one. Simply view them as co-existent evolutionary journeys. The depth of completion of the first one only accelerates the success of the second. The two walk hand-in-hand, each helping the other to grow.

How do you determine what you *really* believe? There is a drastic difference, in my opinion, between what we *really* believe and what we want to believe is true for us. To determine this variance for yourself, ask yourself a couple of questions. How big would you dream if you knew you couldn't fail? Where are you right now? The degree of difference between those two poles tells us what we really believe. Our reactive mind camouflages the truth of what we want until we no longer believe it's possible for us.

Answer the following questions with the first response that comes to mind:

- What kind of love relationship do you want in your life?
- Do you want to be married?
- Do you want children?
- Are you happy?
- Do you like your job?
- What would be your perfect job?
- What would you do if money were no object?
- How much are you worth?
- What's the most important thing in the world to you?
- Who's your best friend?
- What do you dislike about him or her?
- What are you most afraid of?
- Are you close to your family?
- Do you love them?
- Are there any family members or friends whom you resent? Why?
- Do you love yourself?

If you listened carefully to yourself, you probably experienced reactions to certain questions when an answer popped into your mind and then you quickly changed it. That first answer is the *truth.* That is your non-reactive mind speaking with its childlike innocence. When your mind quickly changes, *that* is the facade. That is the reactive mind speaking. That voice contains all the shoulds, oughts and have tos that you have learned through your socialization process. It is the filter that keeps you from seeing, being, doing and having what you really want. When you operated from a position of fear, the reactive mind served a useful purpose. It protected you from events you weren't equipped to handle. However, now that you are dealing with the fears and guilts from the past, the reactive mind only limits your potential. It must be taught to change its habits. It must learn that you are no longer a helpless entity in need of protection. You must get it to quiet down so you can hear the voice of your true beliefs.

A very good friend of mine, Rex Gamble, tells a great story about the voice within. Rex is an internationally known speaker and author of *Believe in Yourself.* While I was attending a meeting at which Rex was the featured speaker, I heard him tell this story:

> *"You'll notice today that I'm wearing a gold pin that reads, #1. That pin was given to me in front of a crowd of 3,000 people by the only man ever written up in the* Guinness Book of World Records *as the world's greatest salesman, Joe Girard. Joe presented me with this pin and said, 'Rex, I want you to wear this pin because you're number one.' Being the kind of person I am, I said, 'Well, thank you, Joe. Yes I am. I didn't know you knew. Thanks!' I went home that day, looked at myself in the mirror and said, 'You're Number One.' Up popped my best friend, Albert. Albert's my little voice within. Albert said, 'Number one what?' I said, 'Albert, I'm the number one salesman in the world.' Albert said, 'No you're not.' I said, 'Albert, I'm the number one speaker in the world today.' Albert said, 'No you're not.' Back and forth we went until finally I took the pin off and sheepishly put it away. I can't argue with Albert, now can I? You see, I couldn't figure out what I was number one at. I didn't put that back*

on for over a year because I couldn't feel like I deserved to wear it. You'll notice I'm wearing it today. No, Albert didn't die. You see, I finally figured out what I'm number one at. I'm the number one Rex Gamble in the whole world. I'm the best me there is."

Find out who the best you is. Determine what you truly believe about yourself and then get on with it. Getting on with it means taking a very clear look at what you want. What do you want to believe about yourself?

The mind has infinite stores beneath its present consciousness.

—William Channing

Are you ready for the tools that will enable you to make a tremendous difference in your life? They are not easy to use because they are so simple. It seems as if things that are simple are for some reason difficult for us to apply and use in our lives. Please don't argue with yourself about these principles until you've tried them in your life. Be consistent. Use them diligently for at least three months. You will never want to go back to living the way you were before. I guarantee it.

Let me give you a $25 million idea.
Take one good idea and use it.

—Andrew Carnegie

There are five principles that have been used by great minds to create the life of their dreams.

1. **Decide specifically what you want.**
2. **Plan for its arrival in your life.**
3. **Act as though you already have it.**
4. **Be patient, diligent and unwavering.**
5. **Accept and acknowledge your good fortune when it comes to you.**

Let's review these powerful principles one at a time.

1. Decide specifically what you want. The law of nature says that what you want, wants you. You just have to allow it to come into your existence. The power of the mind is incredible. All you have to do is decide what you want and then let your mind create it for you. You don't have to know *how* it's going to happen, and oftentimes it will come to you in a form that is totally unexpected. The mind creates solutions for you that are for your highest good, although it might not seem like it to you at the time.

Whether I'm dealing with a relationship goal, a health issue or a financial challenge, I never cease to be amazed at what the mind can create for us. Let me give you a few examples.

A couple of years into our business, my husband and I had a situation where we needed a specific amount of money to help us get past a financial hurdle. We knew how much money we needed, and the situation was getting critical. So we decided that we would go to the bank and get a loan.

As is so often the case, when you really need a loan, the bank doesn't want to give you one, especially if you're self-employed. I was furious as we were leaving our bank after we'd been turned down. We needed that money and we needed it now, not when our financial statement looked better. I ranted and raved all the way home that day about the unfair treatment we had received, how long we'd been good customers of the bank and how dare they treat us in such a manner.

After returning home, we were both in our offices working and my phone rang. On the other end of the line was a new client who had heard about me and wanted me to do some work for them. It was a substantial contract and the last thing the client said to me was, "Is it okay if I overnight the check to you? I want to get this project under way immediately." I was trying to remain cool, calm and collected as I responded with a controlled, "Yes, that would be fine."

What I wanted to do was jump up and down screaming with glee because the check the client was overnighting to me was within pennies of the amount we had just gone to the bank to borrow! You see—what you want, wants you and your mind always works things out for your highest and best good when you're clear about what you want. I thought I needed to get the money from the bank, but my mind knew better. Why borrow money when you can get someone to give it to you?

Another instance that comes to mind had to do with the birth of my son, Andrew. As you know from having read it earlier in the book, I had a very difficult delivery with my daughter, Joy. Consequently, as my pregnancy was progressing with Andrew, I had a feeling of dread about the delivery based on what I'd experienced before. I kept saying, "I don't want to have a delivery like I did last time." I not only said that to my husband and others, but I also said it to myself repeatedly.

There are times when we set goals in our minds and we're not even consciously aware of the chain reaction we've set into motion. The mind takes direction very easily. Therefore, you must be careful about what you say and/or wish for because you just might get it.

Seven days before Andrew's due date, he turned around breech. My doctor tried to manipulate him inside the womb to reposition him and couldn't get him to budge. As a result, I was scheduled for a Caesarean delivery. What a well-kept secret! It doesn't even mess up your makeup. In contrast to the delivery I had had before, a Caesarean was a piece of cake. Do you recognize what took place here? I didn't have a delivery like I'd had before.

There are those who would call both of these situations coincidence. I certainly don't. I've had far too many of these "coincidences" to continue to believe that they were accidental. No, I don't think so. There's something much larger at work in your life once you decide specifically what you want. Thoughts are things and they draw to you the results you desire. Let it work for you. It's a little difficult to arrive at a goal if you don't have one. The mind needs to know what to focus on before it can bring it about. Get very specific about what you want. Your mind will then start making it happen for you, a step at a time.

The mind will create for you that which you focus your energy on. For example, if you want monetary wealth in your life but you're constantly worrying about not having any money, poverty is what you'll get because the mind has been preoccupied with lack of money, not abundance of money. You see, the strongest image wins. The mind is very energy sensitive. If you say you want money but your thoughts are of poverty, the thought patterns are stronger and have more energy in them. Therefore, poverty is what you will get. You must discipline your mind to direct its focus on what you want—not on what you dread. Later I'll give you two techniques to teach your mind how to change its focus from negative to positive, in spite of apparent circumstances. For now, let's focus on the five powerful principles.

2. Plan for the arrival of your desire in your life. In addition to being specific about what you want, you must establish a plan for how you're going to get it. The smaller steps must lead to the larger one. Napoleon Hill, in *Think and Grow Rich,* calls this plan "fixity of purpose."

Write down your long-term goal and work your way backward. Look at the steps you must take to reach that goal. Focus your attention on solutions rather than problems. Each step of the way, look at and recognize your obstacles. Determine how you will overcome them. Set time frames within which you want your accomplishments to occur. Be sure that your intermediate steps support the completion of your long-term goal. Crystallize in your mind what it will take for you to succeed. To keep your life vital, do something every day toward the completion of your plan.

3. Act as though you already have it. In the 1984 Winter Olympics, there was a great deal of talk about the superb performance of certain athletes. These athletes were using revolutionary new techniques of visualization and meditation prior to competing. They saw themselves winning before they actually did. The results were amazing. Although, I'm sure, athletes have used this type of training before, it was the first time it had received a big media splash. Everyone seemed to be talking about it, and the achievements of this particular team were quantum leaps ahead of their competitors, thus undeniable.

You can use that same type of power in your life. Don't underestimate what the mind can do for you. We've heard this over and over again by many famous people of accomplishment. When are we going to listen? What further proof do we need?

The outer world of circumstance shapes itself to the inner world of thought.

—James Allen

After you have decided specifically what you want and made plans to lead you to that end, you should be equipped with some clear mental pictures of what you want. There are two techniques that will rapidly bring your dreams into reality, by helping you to replace negative images in your mind with images of the situation you want to have occur:

1. Using affirmations.
2. Using visualization.

For our purpose here, affirmations are defined as positive statements you say aloud to yourself that are made in the first person, present tense. You use these statements to reprogram the computer of the mind. This is how you change the energy focus from negative to positive. Reprogramming the mind is not simply a matter of saying these things to yourself a couple of times and then getting huge results. The process I'm referring to is a form of personally generated brainwashing. Inundate your mind with thoughts you want it to hold, and after time, it will begin to believe you. It generally requires hundreds of repetitions, augmented by emotional sensations acquired through visualization.

When I began to rebuild my life after I had self-sabotaged it, there were a couple of areas I needed to work on right away. One was finances. I began saying things to myself like, "Creditors can't eat me," and my personal favorite, which came from a Mark Victor Hansen seminar, "I have an overflowing avalanche of abundance in my life right here, right now and I deserve to be rich." The first few times I said that affirmation, I heard a little voice in my head say, "Who are you kidding? An avalanche of abundance? You've barely got enough to make ends meet." After a while, that little voice began to weaken until it finally went away. A funny thing happened once that little voice went away. My financial situation began improving. Hmmmmm, why do you suppose that happened?

Ask and it shall be given unto you.

—Jesus Christ

Affirmations can be used for all kinds of things. For example, I'll share with you the affirmation I used to bring about a loving relationship in my life with the kind of man I wanted.

"I have the perfect man in my life now and we are very much in love. He is older than I am, taller and darker skinned than myself. He is slender and has dark hair. He is a very sophisticated man and enjoys the finer things in life. He appreciates art and music. He's a great dancer and has a wonderful sense of humor. He loves laughter and children. He is strong enough to allow me to be who I am separate from him. He urges me to be the best I can be. We are very happy."

When I first began using this affirmation, this man was not a part of my life, nor was he anywhere to be seen on the horizon. I had stopped dating because my dating experiences were not fulfilling to me. I had spent a lot of time playing the social butterfly. It was not uncommon for me to be dating six to 10 men at a time. All were attractive, successful, intelligent men, but something was missing and I wasn't happy. I began telling myself that I would never get married again. After all, I only like to do things I'm good at and I didn't seem to do marriage well. I joined a health club and got a cat, but something still seemed to be missing.

I knew the power of affirmations and visualization because I had used them on countless other occasions in my life with dramatic success. Once again, I was having a difficult time getting my logical ego out of the way. After all else failed, I decided to use my intuition and mental power to solve my relationships problem.

4. Be patient, diligent and unwavering. I used this affirmation upon arising in the morning and before retiring at night. These are very important times of the day to use your affirmations and visualizations because that's when your mind is the most receptive. Within 60 days, Doug Jones had entered my life from seemingly out of nowhere. He fit my affirmation down to the minute details. You've got to be careful what you ask for because you'll get it.

I'll never forget: One day he was sitting on my sofa after about our third date and he turned to me and said, "Springtime's a nice time to fall in love, don't you think?" He scared me to death. I jumped up and ran into the bathroom and shut the door. I said to myself, "This guy's serious. He's not just dinner and dancing. This guy's talking monogamous relationship!" About that time, I heard a voice in my head say, "What's the matter with you? For the past 60 days, morning and night, you've said your affirmations about the perfect mate you want in your life. Now he's sitting in the living room and here you are in the bathroom. What's the matter with you? Are you crazy?"

With that, I opened the bathroom door, walked out into my living room, and with all the composure I could muster I looked at him and said, "Yes, springtime is a nice time to fall in love."

It was six weeks from the time we started dating until we got married. We have been happily married ever since. Your mind knows how to set up circumstances to bring you your highest good. Had I not been acting as though I already had him in my life, I doubt that he would have arrived upon the scene so quickly, and yet I almost blew it by not recognizing my good fortune when it was delivered to me.

5. Accept and acknowledge your dream when it comes to you. Life with Doug is better than my wildest dreams and I am thankful daily to have him in my life. When we're together, those around us feel our love and energy. It is awesome.

You may be saying to yourself, "That's just a coincidence." Let me tell you that when you've had hundreds of demonstrations like this in your life, as I have, you quit calling it coincidence. Bob Trask says, "A closed mind is more dangerous than a closed parachute. At least a closed parachute kills you instantly." Unless you've got something in your life that brings you better results consistently, don't discount the power of affirmations and visualizations until you've tried using them.

What is a visualization? Visualization is an augmentation of an affirmation. Through visualization you not only say what you want in detail, but you also see it. It has been said that the mind cannot tell the difference between something vividly imagined and something real. This is so true. To change the ruts in your mind, you can use visualization to establish a new set of pictures on which to focus.

In the example of my perfect mate, I saw myself being with this person, experiencing our love and joy, hearing our laughter, feeling his kiss, smelling roses he sent me, etc. This type of sensory visualization convinces your mind that it's real. Therein lies the magic. When your mind believes it's real, it allows it to happen. It accepts it for you and gives it to you.

It's just like the four-minute mile. For years and years few thought the world's record for the four-minute mile could be broken. Many people were convinced that was the fastest possible speed a human could run. This went on for years until one day Roger Bannister broke the record. Shortly after that, several others broke that record. Now it's no big deal. We've got high school kids who can run that fast, let alone Olympians! Get the point? The picture in the mind was the only limiting factor. We've often heard that "believing makes it so." When are we going to trust it? It's simple, but not necessarily easy.

Whether you believe you
can or you can't, either way
you're right.

—Henry Ford

Trying these principles for a little while and then giving up isn't going to get it. It takes staying with the program to produce results in your life. That's where faith and belief come in. You've got to believe that your results are on the way—even if it takes a while.

It just cracks me up when I'm speaking at a seminar and in the center of the room the bullfrogs of negativity are seated, huddled together. I find people's lack of discipline quite amusing. A man said to me once, "Don't give me any of that positive-thinking crap. I tried it once and that stuff just doesn't work." I said, "Oh really, how long did you try it?" to which he responded, "At least four or five days!" I had to refrain from laughing in his face. He was serious and I don't think he had any idea how ridiculous he sounded.

You hold the power within your mind to be, do and have anything you want. However, if you think it's going to come to you in just a couple of days, you're wrong. The good news is, however, that even though it took years for your mind to form its current habits, it will only take a fraction of that time to create a new way of thinking. Some people do it more rapidly than others, depending on the depth of their conviction and their self-discipline.

Give yourself a chance. You owe it to yourself to have everything you want. Use these principles. They have worked for too many others not to work for you as well. Be patient. Allow your crop of new ideas a chance to come to harvest. How many people have you known that quit just as they were on the brink of making it? Don't waste your life that way.

I end this chapter with a quotation by Emmet Fox from his book, *The Mental Equivalent.* He proposes that in order to achieve something new in your life, you must first have a mental picture of the object of desire. He calls that the mental equivalent. It is a truth that has persisted for thousands of years. If you want something present on your physical plane it must first be present on your mental plane. *Change your thought and keep it changed, not for 10 seconds or even 10 days, but steadily and permanently. Supply yourself with a mental equivalent, and the thing must come to you. Without a mental equivalent it cannot come.*

SEVEN

There's a Bump in the Road—So What!

Why can't life's problems hit us
when we're seventeen and
know everything?

—A.C. Jolly

Make the best use of what is in your power, and take the rest as it happens.

—Epictetus

As you travel the path of life it will not be without incident. Learn to welcome these events as opportunities to grow and learn, and you will no longer feel panic-stricken, as if you are experiencing a problem.

One of the most difficult things for us to realize is that we bring many problems on ourselves because of the way we think. "That which we have feared has come upon us" has its root in this type of philosophy. The number of problems that we create in our lives is an indication of how unworthy we feel we are to accomplish our goal and have our good come to us. Learning how to receive is just as important as learning how to give. If we don't really feel we should have our goal, then circumstance will continue to provide all the proof we need to show that we are right. In other words, until you *really believe* that you can have your goal and that you deserve it, you won't get it. Obstacles will always be there to challenge you.

The good news is that once you realize you have the power to change your circumstance, you can get yourself off dead center and get on with your life. It's up to you.

We have nothing to fear but fear itself.

—Franklin D. Roosevelt

When we encounter a problem, we may allow fear to re-enter our lives and regain control. Our fears really don't want to lose the control they have had over us. Sometimes we hold onto our fears because they provide us with a familiar link to our past. When you are new at breaking out of your comfort zone, fear can easily regain control if you're not keeping a watchful eye. However, the more times you are able to repress your fears and move forward, the easier it becomes—and the less often fears arise.

Since we play the starring role in creating our reality by how we think, it's important to put fear into its proper perspective. Fear only raises its ugly head when it is in danger of losing its power over you. As long as you agree to minimize your growth and keep yourself within your comfortable rut, there is no reason for fear to escalate. However, when you peek out of that rut and reach beyond your previous experiences, you may set off the alarms. These alarms are triggered by anxious feelings. Your feelings of anxiety will tend to escalate as you get closer to meeting your goal. Keep that in mind and know that you are very close to winning!

The more comfortable you become with hurdling ruts, the less likely you will be to encounter the obstacles created by fear. Those obstacles may still be there, but your perception of them will be different. The problems won't seem as ominous for you.

The ones who try to do something and fail are infinitely better than those who try to do nothing and succeed.

—Lloyd Jones

There will be people in your life who will be standing in the wings just waiting for you to fail. They are the ones who told you how crazy you were for pursuing your dream in the first place. Although they probably wouldn't admit it to themselves, they really *want* you to fail so they can be proved right. They love to say, "I told you so." Be prepared for those individuals and don't let them upset you or take away any of your momentum. Try to keep in mind that their "I told you so's" help them to feel competent.

Viewed from that perspective, you can allow their input to roll off you like water off a duck's back. Their world is so small. Grant them the pleasure of their I told you so's, and you will negate its effect. It will be evident to them that their words are powerless over you, but they won't know *for sure* if you've noticed it too. This allows them to save face and it really doesn't cost you anything unless you choose to let it.

It should be evident to you by now that life is really not all that serious. In reality, there is very little in this world that should be allowed to disturb us or cause us to alter our dreams. Life, and the way we respond to it, is truly just a matter of perspective. If you know where you're going and have a picture in your mind of what being there is going to be like, you'll make it. In the broader scope of our purpose in life, problems we encounter are really nothing more than bothersome details. When you can view the world from that position, you have your ego under control. By so doing, you will have a peace and a joy in your life that many people will envy but few will understand.

Experience is a name everyone gives to their mistakes.

—Oscar Wilde

Experience seems to imply wisdom gained. When we are confronted with difficulty, it is wise for us to discover the lesson therein. To deny the existence of such lessons will only cause a similar situation to reappear in our lives later. This is how we create repetitious mistakes and a spiral of frustration.

Have you ever been in an unpleasant situation in which you said to yourself, "I'm never going to do this again"? The next thing you know, you are confronted with a similar problem and you react in the same manner. Of course, afterwards you say, "That was absolutely the last time," but it's not, and the cycle continues. Have you ever wondered why things like this seem to happen to you over and over again?

The law of the Universe brings us opportunities for mistakes in our lives so that we may learn the lessons they contain. If we choose not to learn the lesson, however, it will re-create itself in our lives until we finally get the message. Once the lesson is learned we can move on, but not before.

I have a friend who perpetuates a problem of alcoholism in her life. Her father was an alcoholic. She bought into feeling sorry for him and assisted him in validating the "poor victim" role he had designed for himself. Although she was quite vocal regarding her hatred for that situation, she *married* a man who was an alcoholic. Again she felt sorry for him and his victim position. He needed her to help him be strong and although she professed to despise the situation, she was still there. Eventually that marriage dissolved. When she began to date again, the man she chose drank heavily. They married and again, much to her surprise (although not to anyone else's), she discovered he was an alcoholic. The cycle repeated. It seemed to be evident to everyone but her. This time there was a new dimension. She felt that if she left him he would die. She had finally reached a point of feeling *responsible* for the life or death of someone.

Until she comes to grips with why it is so vitally important for her to feel so intensely needed, she will continue to surround herself with powerless individuals who *need* her strength. Therefore, this pattern will continue in her life until she learns those lessons.

It's so easy to see a negative pattern forming in someone else's life, but it isn't quite as clear to us when viewing our own. It is imperative, then, for us to keep a keen awareness. When you experience a problem, don't gloss it over and be on your way. Be sure to locate the root of the problem and deal with it. Determine if you have experienced something like it before. See the pattern and stop it. Otherwise, it will return again and again. When you make repetitious mistakes, it is a waste of your energy and life. Learn your lessons well and expend your energy on your positive path to growth. We have gone overboard with the "Everyone needs to be needed" routine. Isn't it more accurate to say that everyone wants to be desired? If we accept that, we avoid the destructive forces of need—which imply desperation.

The world is round and the place which may seem like the end may also be only the beginning.

—Ivy Baker Priest

As troubles come our way it seems to be human nature for us to turn inward and begin to doubt ourselves. This can rob us of the enthusiasm with which we pursue our goals. If you feel discouraged you can:

- Re-focus on your dream and why it's important to achieve it.
- Seek support from your Master Mind group.
- Review your steps of accomplishment toward your goal.
- Reward yourself for your endeavors.
- Continue to take one step each day toward your goal.
- Get involved in a project outside of yourself.

It always helps you to view your situation in a better light when you can assist those less fortunate than yourself.

An understanding that problems arise to teach you something, rather than to destroy you, can help you maintain a high level of confidence. Problems often come into our lives to keep us on track rather than wandering off. If you've been following your dream and things are going smoothly, you may decide to branch off in a new direction. That's wonderful. It shows that risk is less of a threat for you. However, if this new direction is heavily laden with problems, it may be the Universe telling you that this is not the way to go. Be aware and listen to your intuition, for it is always right.

We learn courageous action by going forward whenever fear or difficulty urges us back. A little boy was asked how he learned to skate. "Oh, by getting up every time I fell down," he answered. We can pick ourselves up, too.

EIGHT

Do It Now!

Things don't turn up
in this world until somebody
turns them up.

—James A. Garfield

The only joy in the world is to begin.

—Cesare Pavese

All the planning, calculating and strategizing in the world are no substitute for taking action. Graveyards are filled with people who *were* going to achieve their dreams *someday*. Don't go to the grave with your music still in you. Let it out. Share it with the world now.

Many people suffer from analysis paralysis. If you are one of them, you spend your life waiting for just the "right" time to take your plunge. By waiting, you cheat yourself out of your life. This is the only chance you've got. Make it count. It has often been said that you don't have to begin to fail, but you have to begin to succeed. What are you waiting for?

There is only one thing about which I'm certain, and this is that there is very little about which one can be certain.

—W. Somerset Maugham

There is no way of knowing, prior to going toward your dream, that you will make it. If it were somehow possible to give ourselves that guarantee, there would be no risk. People would be performing at amazing levels of capacity because they wouldn't feel fear. Therefore, it wouldn't limit them and their thinking. "How big would you dream if you knew you couldn't fail?" I hope you can see that the only thing preventing you from having what you want is a little old thing called fear. Bite by bite, step by step, anything can be conquered. The trick is to understand that we don't need guarantees because we don't need to be afraid of failing.

What you think is what you are. Just look at a bumblebee, for example. From an engineering standpoint it is not *physically* possible for the bumblebee to fly—its body is too heavy. Its wings cannot *physically* support it in flight. There's a problem, though. I think someone forgot to tell the bumblebees! Someone forgot to tell them it can't be done. They believe that they can fly, and so they do.

Forget to tell yourself the things that have been holding you back. Only tell yourself "can do" thoughts. It will surprise you at what will start taking place. It was Diane De Poitiers who said, "Courage is as often the outcome of despair as of hope; in the one case we have nothing to lose, in the other everything to gain." Let your courage come to you through your hopes and your dreams. Trust yourself. You'll come through with flying colors.

To achieve great things, we must live as if we were never going to die.

—Vauvenargues

The following is a condensed version of each chapter and the primary thought it holds.

Confusion Is the Prelude to Clarity

You don't have to know everything in order to create the life of your dreams. All you have to know is the first step and be open to life's direction.

Hello in There

You must get a good fix on where you are now, for it is your starting point.

Dreams Are the Stuff from Which Reality Is Made

Encourage yourself to dream. Push yourself to your limits. Don't settle for less than you can truly be.

At the Fork in the Road?

You can't get what you want until you know what you want. Really look for the direction, listen to your inner voice and it will become clear to you.

Using Guilt as Your Guide

Cut loose from the past. You don't live there anymore. Growing isn't always easy, but it's always worth it.

You Are Everything You Need

Focus is powerful and important. Consider for a moment that the sun doesn't generally burn grass or paper, but put it through a magnifying glass and you have a fire. Your power is increased the same way. Focus makes your energy awesome and enables you to create the life of your dreams.

There's a Bump in the Road—So What!

Don't let anything keep you from your dreams. You are not weak, so don't pretend you are.

Do It Now!

There is no time like the present—so go for it!

Fear created gods;
boldness created kings.

—Prosper Jalyot

The power that rests in you rests in us all. Be yourself and fulfill your potential. Don't let anyone rain on your parade.

Let the music begin!

Suggested Reading

Bach, M. *The World of Serendipity*. Marina del Rey, CA: DeVorss & Co., 1980.

Bach, R. *Jonathan Livingston Seagull. New York: AvonBooks*, 1976.

Brown, L. *Live Your Dreams*. New York: William Morrow & Co., 1992.

Butterworth, E. *Spiritual Economics—The Prosperity Process*. Unity Village, MO: Unity School of Christianity, 1983.

Chopra, D. *Creating Affluence*. San Rafael, CA: New World Library, 1993.

———. *The Seven Spiritual Laws of Success*. SanRafael, CA: New World Library, 1995.

Cole-Whittaker, T. *How to Have More in a Have Not World*. New York: Fawcett Books, 1985.

———. *What You Think of Me Is None of My Business*. La

Jolla, CA: Oak Tree Publications, 1982.

de Angelis, B. *Real Moments*. New York: Delacorte Press, 1994.

Gerber, M.E. *E-Myth: Why Most Small Businesses Still Don't Work and What to Do About Yours*. New York: HarperBusiness, 1995.

Hansen, M.V. *Future Diary*. Costa Mesa, CA: Mark Victor Hansen & Associates.

Hansen, M.V. & Canfield, J. *Chicken Soup for the Soul*. Deerfield Bch., FL: Health Communications, Inc., 1993.

Hill, N. *Think and Grow Rich*. New York: Fawcett Crest Books, 1987.

Johnson, S. *One Minute for Myself: How to Manage Your Most Valuable Asset*. New York: Avon, 1987.

Kinnear, W. *Thirty-Day Mental Diet*. Marina del Ray, CA: DeVorss & Co., 1990.

Kinnear, W. & Holmes, E. *How to Change Your Life*. Los Angeles, CA: Science of Mind Publications, 1982.

Kragen, K. & Graham, J. *Life Is a Contact Sport: The Ten Point Strategy to Turbo-Charge Your Career*. New York: William Morrow & Co.

Loehr, J.E. *Mental Toughness Training*. New York: N.A.L. Dutton, 1991.

MacKay, H. *Swim with the Sharks Without Being Eaten Alive: Outsell, Outmanage, Outmotivate & Outnegotiate Your Competition*. New York: William Morrow & Co., 1988.

Maltz, M. *Psycho-Cybernetics.* Hollywood, CA: Wilshire, 1973.

Mandino, O. *The Greatest Salesman in the World*. New York: Bantam Books, 1983.

McWilliams, P. & JR. *Do It! Let's Get Off Our Butts*. LosAngeles, CA: Prelude Press, 1992.

Melton, J. *Your Right to Fly.* Palm Springs, CA: Global Publications, 1979.

Millman, D. *Way of the Peaceful Warrior: A Book that Changes Lives*. Tiburon, CA: H.J. Kramer, Inc., 1984.

Ponder, C. *The Millionaire from Nazareth.* Marina del Rey, CA: DeVorss & Co., 1979.

Pritchett, P. *The Quantum Leap Strategy.* Dallas, TX: Pritchett & Associates, 1991.

Robbins, A. *Awaken the Giant Within: How to Take Immediate Control of Your Emotional, Physical and Financial Destiny.* New York: Simon & Schuster, 1992.

Trask, B. *God's Phone Number*. Issaquah, WA: ARAS Publishing, 1987.

About the Author

Debra Jones is a classic example of today's entrepreneur . . . wife, mother and owner of a multimillion-dollar business. She's learned how to not only be a success in business, but also a success in life. According to Debra, "A successful business and a successful life don't have to be mutually exclusive. You can have both!"

Debra is a household name with the mortgage banking industry, where she has worked for the last several years. Her client list reads like a "Who's Who" of that industry and ranges from small companies to multibillion-dollar corporations.

She is the author of several bestselling audio and video cassette programs, author and publisher of three newsletters read by tens of thousands throughout the United States, Canada, Australia and Puerto Rico, and has created an entire catalog of sales and marketing tools designed to increase levels of success in business.

Outside the mortgage industry, she travels the country extensively presenting her powerful message to thousands of business people every year, which is a testament to what one can achieve when they set their mind to it, are willing to work hard and never, never give up on their dreams, in spite of the many setbacks along the way. It's a message she delivers with passion because it's a page from her life. Starting from ground zero, but with a great idea and a lot of enthusiasm, she built her business into a multi-million-dollar empire in less than 10 years.

Debra is one of the most dynamic, entertaining and "content rich" speakers on the platform today. You can contact Debra by calling 1-800-456-1001.

Order Form

Phone Orders:
800-456-1001 or
918-341-8782

Fax Orders:
918-342-2324

Postal Orders:
Hark & Associates
225 S. Brady
Claremore, OK 74017

	Each	Quantity	Amount
From Thin Air To Millionaire™ *(book)*	$11.95	____	_____
What You Want, Wants You *(book)*	$11.95	____	_____
Teach Yourself to Sell *(6 tape audio series)*	$99.00	____	_____
Creating Market Dominance *(4 tape audio series)*	$75.00	____	_____
		Sub Total	_____
(add 9 % for products shipped to OK addresses)		**Sales Tax**	_____
(U.S. add $3 per product)		**Shipping & Handling**	_____
		Total	_____

Ship To:

Name ____

Address ____

City ____________________________ State ______ Zip ________

Phone ____________________ E-mail ______________________

Payment Type: ❑ Check / Money Order ❑ Credit Card

❑ VISA ❑ Mastercard ❑ American Express ❑ Discover

Credit Card # ____________________________________

Name on card ___________________________ Exp. date ________

Signature _______________________________________